Fighting Chance
The autobiography of Irfon Williams

Fighting Chance

The Autobiography of Irfon Williams

Ed.: Nia Roberts
Translated by Geraint Løvgreen

Gwasg Carreg Gwalch

First publication: 2018
© Irfon Williams Estate/Gwasg Carreg Gwalch

ISBN: 978-1-84527-677-5

Published with the financial support
of the Welsh Books Council

Cover design: Eleri Owen
Cover photo kindly received from ITV/*O'r Galon*,
with special thanks to Sian Morgan Lloyd and Rhys Edwards
Other photos kindly received from the family, Mel Parry, Arwyn Roberts
and Eryl Crump, Trinity Mirror/*Daily Post* papers

Published by Gwasg Carreg Gwalch,
12 Iard yr Orsaf, Llanrwst, Wales LL26 0EH
tel: 01492 642031
email: books@carreg-gwalch.cymru
website: www.carreg-gwalch.cymru

Printed and published in Wales

For Becky

Thank you, Becky. Thank you for everything.
I love you more than you'll ever know.

Foreword

Irfon asked me if I would write an introduction to his autobiography, but now, as I sit here writing what feels like an 'afterword', my beloved husband Irfon has gone forever. He was determined to finish this book so that his story might be remembered, as a record of his life, for his children especially.

In January 2014 we were living life to the full, both of us working in the field of children and young people's mental health, and busy parents to our two little boys. Suddenly, our world was turned upside down when Irfon learned that he had bowel cancer and that the condition was quite advanced in his body, even though he was only 43 years old.

This is the autobiography of a loving husband, a proud father of five and a true Welshman. He spent two years writing it, and completed the job from his bed just a few days before his death. It's a very personal story, in which Irfon recounts his cancer journey, his childhood and the experiences that influenced his life – the experiences that made my husband such a brave and charismatic man. *Fighting Chance* is a record of his life and his humour, a record of the elation and heartbreak that followed the treatments he received, and a record of his determination to survive cancer whilst taking on the political system in Wales.

My world was shattered when Irfon died on 30 May 2017 in Ysbyty Gwynedd in Bangor. We were happiest when together, and hated being apart. Although Irfon's battle was a public one, it ended very privately, and we were both sitting together holding hands when he took his last breath.

Through his words, and those of people who made the journey alongside him, here's Irfon's story – a document of how he became an inspiration to so many throughout Wales. It's a story of how the strength of love kept him alive against the odds, a story of his battle to secure the right to live, and proof that despite everything he managed to smile and find joy in every day.

I can't describe the pride I feel that I was able to spend ten happy years with Irfon. We were a solid, devoted partnership: he was my best friend, my biggest supporter and always made me feel completely adored. I have the gift of two sons in which he lives on.

Diolch i ti, Irfs, am bob dim. Caru ti am byth xxx

Rebecca Williams
November 2017

Chapter 1

Diagnosis

Monday 28 January 2014 was a cold, misty, grey day. I'd been waiting for a phone call from Meinir Williams, manager of the Betsi Cadwaladr Health Board operational department, and the phone rang shortly after lunchtime.

'The doctor's ready to meet you at four o'clock this afternoon, Irfon,' she said. 'He wants to give you the diagnosis.'

From working in the health service myself, I knew that Meinir would be aware of the diagnosis, so I asked her to tell me there and then. She refused, but invited us up to her office in person, so off we went straight away to Meinir's office at Ysbyty Gwynedd, our local hospital.

Walking into the office was quite a weird experience. I saw two or three girls I knew – Meinir's colleagues – and I suspect they had an inkling of what I was about to hear. Becky, my wife, and I knew Meinir well, and to her credit, she didn't beat about the bush and try to make small talk before discussing the important business. As soon as we'd sat down, Meinir told us exactly what the diagnosis was.

'Irfon, you've got advanced bowel cancer and metastases in the liver.'

The words felt as if I'd been hit in the face with a frying pan. I felt an enormous shock, as if time had frozen for a second or two; but to be perfectly honest, I don't know why I was so shocked, because the news wasn't unexpected.

I'd intended to meet Yvonne Harding, my manager at work, that afternoon on the hospital children's ward, but Meinir phoned her first, and she immediately rushed to the operational department to see me. She swore when she heard the news, before saying, 'It's not good news then!'. As you'd expect, Becky was in tears, but for some reason I didn't cry – Meinir, Becky and Yvonne thought I was in shock, but really I felt as if I had quite a good grip on the situation. Having the diagnosis confirmed was a relief, to be honest, and was much easier than the awful feeling of waiting for the result. At least I knew now what the problem was, and was ready to learn what could be done about it.

By four o'clock we were in Llandudno Hospital. Meinir, fair play to her, had arranged to meet us there, and we were shortly joined by the consultant, Mr Bhalerao, to confirm what Meinir had said earlier that afternoon. In the short time since he'd learnt that we were on our way to him, he'd managed to discuss my case with the cancer doctors and had arranged an appointment for me with them in a fortnight's time on the Alaw unit at Ysbyty Gwynedd.

Mr Bhalerao explained that I'd need a course of chemotherapy to start with, followed by a course of radiotherapy, before they'd consider operating. The message, then, was a positive one. In a way, that meeting brought an end to a very difficult month of looking for answers, dealing with symptoms and going through unpleasant tests, and I was very grateful to Mr Bhalerao for making time to meet us – and to Meinir, of course, for her support.

I'd better take you back a bit now, to December 2013, to give you the whole background. I was with Becky and our sons, Siôn Arwyn and Ianto Huw, aged four and two at the time, on a short break at Center Parcs up in Cumbria – a chance to relax as a family before the Christmas rush and, of course, a break from work. Lately I'd been under increasing pressure in my role as Manager of Children and Young People's Mental Health Services within Betsi Cadwaladr Health Board, and a few people

The boys and I in Center Parcs

had told me that I didn't look well – that I looked tired. While we were at Center Parcs I became constipated and as a result felt uncomfortable with pains in my stomach. Despite constantly going back and forth to the toilet, I wasn't having much success – which was a whole new experience for me. To tell you the truth, going to the toilet had often been a bone of contention when I was growing up as I used to play that old trick of going immediately after mealtimes rather than stay to help wash the dishes!

I remember talking about it with Becky after the boys had gone to bed, and we agreed that it was a sign of stress, due to my current situation at work. We discussed cancer too, and persuaded ourselves that that was impossible, as I wasn't showing any signs of the obvious symptoms like bleeding.

On arriving home from Center Parcs I made an appointment to see the doctor. It was a locum that I saw, a few days later – a very nice lady who agreed that stress was the most probable explanation. But just to be on the safe side, she arranged blood tests for me, and asked me to provide a stool sample. Off I went with a prescription for a laxative, to help me carry out the task.

A week flew by quite quickly, and back I went to see the doctor again. The tests were all fine and nothing appeared amiss, but the laxative hadn't helped much so the dose was doubled and I went home. Now my bowels were functioning but the constipated feeling was still there. Later, I learnt that it was the tumour in the bowel that was creating the feeling of needing to go to the toilet, so in fact being constipated wasn't as much of a problem as I'd thought. Christmas passed by without any fuss – we had fun as usual, and I managed to forget about my predicament, more or less.

The doctor wanted to see me again during the first week of January, to assess any change in my condition. By now I was suffering from pain in my chest and ribs, which was quite bad at times. I was given an ECG, a heart test, by a nurse, but the results of that were fine, so they decided to send me to hospital for a scan. A few days later I received a letter confirming an appointment in the X-ray department.

Of course, by then I'd gone back to work and had mentioned to my manager, Yvonne, that I was having the tests. She'd been really supportive and had assured me that I didn't need to worry about work at all. On the morning of the scan – it was a Thursday – I was meant to attend a meeting in Wrexham at 9 a.m. I sent my apologies; by that time I'm sure the team there suspected that something was wrong, as I'd missed a number of meetings, and everyone knew how conscientious I usually was. But at the time, I wasn't bothered about work (which was a strange feeling) as sorting out my health was far more important. Although I was going in to work, my heart wasn't in it.

They did an ultrasound scan of my stomach, and I

remember asking the woman operating the scanner if she could see anything suspicious. Her matter-of-fact answer was 'Your GP will contact you with the results'. Although I'm quite aware that staff aren't allowed to divulge results during the test, I had a bad feeling about it. I was quite right too, as within minutes of arriving back at the office in Bangor, a little over thirty minutes after the scan, I got a telephone call from a receptionist at our GP's surgery. The doctor wanted to see me at four o'clock that afternoon – obviously, the scan result had already arrived, and I guessed that the news awaiting me was bad.

I remember that the doctor was surprised to see me there without anyone to support me, but Siôn had a hospital appointment that day, and Becky had taken him. So I was on my own when I found out that the scan had shown something on my liver and right kidney. There were two lesions on the liver and one on the kidney. I asked the obvious question: what were they? Without making any commitment, the doctor said that all possibilities needed to be examined and that cancer was obviously one of them.

I felt the tears start to well up – not because of the news and what that meant for me, but from thinking of how it would affect Becky and my parents. Before getting into the car, I phoned Becky to tell her the news. Naturally, she was upset, and I too found it impossible to hold back the tears. I drove straight home to her, and it was so good to feel her arms around me, holding me tight. We had a long talk, and decided to remain positive until we knew for certain what was wrong. Whatever the situation, the two of us would fight it together.

That evening I phoned my friend Big Kev, who's a very experienced radiographer. Kev was honest with us, fair play to him, saying that cancer was a possibility, of course, but that the lesions could be scars resulting, perhaps, from years of playing rugby or the car accident I'd been in with Mam and Arwyn, my brother, when I was ten years old.

The doctor referred me urgently to the hospital's surgical department, which meant that I would receive an appointment letter within fourteen days. That may not sound a long time, but it felt like an eternity at the time, and I've learnt from experience that waiting is one of the hardest things to do. I let Yvonne know that I wouldn't be at work regularly for a while, until I found out exactly what my situation was.

I decided to take advantage of the fact that I've worked in the Health Service for years. I wasn't afraid to question and knock on doors to search for answers, and I was in Ysbyty Gwynedd before 10 the next morning, looking for the departmental secretaries' room. I saw Gail, a woman I knew as a former colleague from years ago, who explained the procedure to me: the doctors would discuss the referral and then decide who would be dealing with the case. They weren't due to meet until the following week, but on seeing how anxious I was, Gail took my phone number, saying that she'd talk to the coordinator.

Less than an hour later I received a call from the coordinator, saying that a surgeon named Mr Bhalerao had agreed to take my case, and that he'd be sending me an appointment. I was extremely grateful to her, and to the doctor – but for some reason, and against my nature to be honest, I was like a maniac, desperate to sort everything out. Now that I knew the name of the surgeon who'd be treating me, I went back to the hospital to introduce myself to his secretary, apologising for being so forward and asking when the appointment would be. As she hadn't yet had an opportunity to talk to Mr Bhalerao she couldn't give me an answer, but she said she'd call me later that afternoon.

The end of the afternoon came and I'd heard nothing, so up I went again to look for answers. When I got to Mr Bhalerao's office the door was open, and the man himself was sat in the corner of the room, looking at me in astonishment!

After a brief conversation, he arranged to see me the following Thursday for a full consultation, and I suggested that it would be a good idea for him to order the necessary scans there and then, to get the ball rolling, as it were. He was a bit shocked, I'm sure, at my cheek, but he agreed to do so. He got out a form, wrote down my details and what was needed on it, and off I went to hassle the staff in the X-ray department.

The scan appointment came very quickly, but first I had to see Mr Bhalerao. Becky came with me to that appointment, in the Ysbyty Gwynedd Outpatients' Department. If I'd known what awaited me there I would have run away as fast as I could! Mr Bhalerao needed to assess me, so he asked me to explain my symptoms. I explained everything – by now I'd started to lose weight too. He pushed and prodded my stomach, and said that I had a hernia. For a few seconds I remember being relieved that it was only a hernia, but of course, that was just a coincidence.

The next part of the examination was unpleasant, to say the least. Mr Bhalerao asked me to lie down on my side and raise my legs up to my chest. He explained that he'd be putting cold gel on my bottom, which felt a bit uncomfortable. He inserted a finger (or fingers – I don't know) into my back passage, and I was very proud of myself for coping so well with the treatment. But when I saw the nurse open a package and take out the most terrifying piece of equipment I've ever seen, I nearly fainted! It was evident what was afoot, and before I could turn around the long, white contraption had disappeared into a place where the sun had never shone! I very nearly jumped, and I'm sure I emitted terrible noises. I remember Becky, from behind the curtain, asking me over and over again if I was alright. Mr Bhalerao had warned me that I'd feel a rather painful pulling sensation ... he wasn't joking!

After the examination, he said he'd found something that he didn't like the look of, but that he hadn't been able to take a good enough sample of it. I nearly fainted when he announced that I'd have to go to the endoscopy department the following afternoon for a camera examination, and for him to extract an adequate sample of whatever it was that he'd seen. Although Mr Bhalerao hadn't confirmed that it was cancer, it was fairly obvious to me what the outcome would be. I was really pleased to see a friendly, familiar face come through the door – Lowri, a Specialist Bowel Nurse, bringing me a cup of tea.

The next day Becky and I went anxiously up to the endoscopy department, and sat in a pretty grim waiting room. A nurse came to take my details and explain the process in detail to me, before handing me the most ridiculous pair of underpants I've ever seen, big blue ones with a hole in the back, obviously to allow access for the camera. I put on a kind of

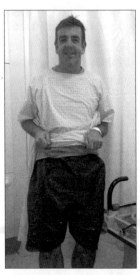

gown too, one that was done up at the back, but before putting on the underpants I had to have an enema. As the nurse knew me (I'd worked in Ysbyty Gwynedd for many years) she asked if I was happy for her to give me the enema. Of course, I had no objection, especially after she said that she'd heated it up nicely for me.

If you've ever had an enema, you'll know how difficult and uncomfortable it is to hold it in for a short period, let alone fifteen minutes! I think I lasted about ten minutes, and I have to admit that having such a good bowel movement, after weeks of sitting on the toilet in vain, was a great feeling! I was offered medication to make me sleepy and relaxed, and considering the previous day's experience I was only too eager to accept.

The lovely underpants

So off I went to the treatment room where two doctors and a team of nurses were waiting for me. Becky stayed in the waiting room. By that time, the doctors didn't feel that I needed the sedative after all, and I agreed to that, as gas and air was available should I feel any pain.

I'm very pleased to say that the camera wasn't half as uncomfortable as the previous day's treatment. Nevertheless, it wasn't a very pleasant experience. I had a look around the room as the doctor got down to it, and saw a trainee nurse named Lois standing beside me.

'I remember you lecturing me at University last year,' she said to me – and the ensuing discussion we had about that was quite a surreal experience, bearing in mind that I had a camera at the end of a pipe up my backside at the time!

At the end of the test Mr Bhalerao once again wouldn't confirm anything, but he did admit that what he'd seen wasn't normal. I was taken to a room to relax. Becky was waiting for me. During the test, Mr Bhalerao had had to pump air into the bowel (a very uncomfortable feeling), and of course, that had to go somewhere. Picture me, in my big blue underpants and gown, with a terrible bellyache, nearly dying to break wind. All my life the women in my life – especially Mam and Becky – have turned their noses up when I've broken wind, but the nurses had a quite different attitude. They, and Becky, following their lead, urged me to do it, and I'll never forget the words of one nurse: 'Let rip a proper fart and you'll be a new man!' Everything settled down pretty well after that, and we went home.

The next week I was due to have a CT scan – the first of many. I have to say, I've been treated wonderfully by the staff at Ysbyty Gwynedd's X-ray department, and have admired the care given to other patients too. After the scan I remember seeing an old friend of mine who works in the cancer deprtment, Nerys Haf, who asked me what I was doing there. I told her everything. Without warning, Nerys started to cry, and I don't know why, but I started crying with her. And there we both were for a few minutes, hugging each other through our tears. That was a very therapeutic experience actually – although Nerys, bless her, felt a bit awkward afterwards.

The results of the tests arrived at Mr Bhalerao's office the following week, ready for him to give us the diagnosis.

* * *

After the diagnosis, the task of talking to family and friends was a difficult one. Obviously, Mam and Clive (her husband), Dad, Becky's parents, and Gary, my best friend, had been very supportive, and we'd shared everything with them, step by step. Even so, accepting the diagnosis was very difficult for all of them. I felt for my parents, who had already lost one son, my brother Arwyn – death tends to spring to the forefront of the mind when discussing cancer, doesn't it? Everyone was terribly upset, but I was keen to encourage them to be as positive as possible, as Becky and I were adamant that that was the only way we could deal with the situation.

But another difficult task faced me. The next morning, I had to phone my ex-wife, Lisa, to discuss how to talk to – and support – my three older children, Lois, Owen and Beca. Since separating we hadn't been able to communicate with each other very well at all, unfortunately, but it was even more important now that we talked, for the sake of the children. It was obviously a massive shock for her, and she asked if she could phone me back. About ten minutes later we had a discussion about how to break the news to them. I was anxious to tell them as soon as possible in case they heard from anyone else, and Lisa agreed to break the news that night after the three arrived home from school and college. I spoke with her again the next day, and she explained then that the children had been awfully upset, as was to be expected. I arranged to take them out for a meal that evening, as it was important for them to know that I hadn't changed at all. I wanted them to see that I was thinking positively – and that the Dad who said and did stupid things was still as embarrassing as ever!

When I went to pick them up I got the usual welcome. I explained briefly that I'd undergone tests before the diagnosis, including a camera up my backside. To lighten the situation I started to joke about financial cuts in the NHS meaning that I had to take my own (very big) camera in with me but that they needn't worry because I'd cleaned it afterwards with baby wipes! Owen and Beca, who were 16 and 13 at the time, didn't

Becky and I with all the children, August 2011

want to ask any questions but Lois, at eighteen, was desperate to know everything. I tried to emphasise how important it was for them to share their worries, and that I'd be on hand to answer as many of their questions as possible.

Talking to friends was just as hard. Becky phoned some of our friends to tell them, and I opened up to two close friends – Alan Owen and John Burns – asking them to pass the news on to the rest of the lads. I remember phoning Robbie, my friend since we were 13 years old, and a rugby team-mate. Robbie's a bit of a character, always playing pranks and joking, so after telling him the diagnosis I asked him if he knew of any good wig shops, for the time when I'd be losing my hair. He didn't find it funny, and the next morning I was in tears reading a letter that Robbie had posted through my letterbox. Having said that, Robbie and his brother, Richie, have since been a breath of fresh air with their sense of humour, and both have been really supportive.

Although I remained positive most of the time there were tough periods too. I didn't cry much, except with Becky, but sometimes my mind would turn to very dark places. That was worst during the night – I'd be lying in bed, unable to sleep and imagining what would happen if I died. Would the children be ok? How would Lois, Owen and Beca cope? Would Siôn and Ianto remember me, them being so young? How would Becky carry on without me? What effect would this have on my parents? I'd try to persuade myself that everyone would be fine, that Becky was more than capable of looking after the boys and that she'd tell them stories about me forever ... and of course, there were hundreds of photos of me for them to look back at. Dad might struggle initially, but Becky would make sure that his relationship with the children – Siôn and Ianto, in particular – remained strong, as she knows how important that is to me. Clive would support Mam and she'd understand too that I'd want her to be there for all the children. Mam has a group of very good friends and I know they'd be very supportive of her, as they have been during my illness.

I also remember thinking about my funeral, for some reason – thinking that I wouldn't want it to be a sad occasion, which is obviously a stupid thought. What music would I want? I downloaded some of our favourite songs and pondered which ones would be suitable and make people smile as they remembered me. I'd have one hymn, maybe – 'Calon Lân' would be the obvious one. Thinking like this made me smile because some of my ideas were totally inappropriate. I wasn't ready to die either, and when I contemplated that, the positive attitude would take over and I'd be able to fall asleep quite easily.

* * *

In no time at all, countless messages started arriving – by telephone, e-mail, cards, letters etc. It was incredible how many people contacted me, and offered their support.

Shortly, I was given an appointment with Chas, a Specialist Chemotherapy Nurse at Ysbyty Gwynedd. Manon Ogwen, a manager at Alaw cancer unit, who's also a friend of mine, came to meet us at the unit at the same time. Chas was really friendly and an important point of contact in the early days. He was particularly good at describing what was going to happen to me, the effect of the treatment and so on. He took us around the unit so that I could see where I'd be receiving the treatment, and introduced me to some of the nurses who'd be looking after me. Everyone appeared very friendly and the atmosphere there was much happier than expected. I felt a lot happier after hearing the details of the treatment, and was keen to get started, but one very important thing needed to be done first.

Although Becky and I had been together a while, and had the two little ones, we hadn't had time to think about getting married, though we'd often talked about it. I was intending to ask Becky to marry me that summer anyway, and we both agreed that we wanted to face the battle ahead of us as husband and wife. After discussing it, Becky and I decided to arrange a quiet registry office wedding with the children, our parents and our best friends as witnesses. The problem with this, of course, was that a number of people who are important to us would be left out – principally Becky's grandparents, or Nana and Daido as she calls them. Despite being almost in their nineties they're very healthy, and Siôn and Ianto have been privileged to cultivate a close relationship with their great grandparents. I think the world of them too. And Becky's parents, Dylan and Glenna, weren't about to let their only daughter get married without having a day to remember, and so the wedding grew in size.

There wasn't much for me to do except invite family, buy a suit and pick a best man. The only thing missing was the stag night – and thank goodness for that! Over the years, I'd been on various stag trips with friends, mainly the rugby boys, and it was always my role to be the judge in some ridiculous 'court', penalising people for breaking silly rules such as only drinking with the left hand. The groom himself, poor thing, would be dressed up in the most ridiculous costumes ... and I'm sure a lot of the lads would have loved to see me have to suffer the same treatment.

During that period I spent a lot of time at home looking after Siôn and Ianto while Becky was out with her mother arranging the wedding. They did most of the work, but I did go to Chester with Becky on the Monday afternoon before the wedding to buy myself a suit. After trying many suits on, however, I found that none of them were suitable. They were all too long, too short or too wide. A shop assistant hovered around us with a tape measure around his neck, making a bit of a nuisance of himself, to be honest. He insisted that any suit could be altered to fit, but when I explained to him that I was getting married the following Thursday he looked at me quite crossly. 'Well, that's ridiculous, you've left it far too late,' he said. The poor chap didn't know which way to turn when Becky started crying, and I had to explain to him why she was in such a state!

I was adamant from the outset that my best friend, Gary, would be my best man, and he bought the same suit as me to ensure that we looked smart in the photographs. We needed a photographer, and Mel Parry, one of my friends at Benllech Rugby Club where I'd coached for a while, was a professional photographer. (One of the good things about playing rugby is that you make friends for life, as

Our wedding day

people from all walks of life play together in harmony). Although his diary was full he went out of his way to arrange things so that he could be there, and he took excellent pictures for us. I felt proud of myself for completing my tasks – before realising how busy Becky had been in the meantime!

I took a call one day from Wally, one of the first team members at Bangor Rugby Club, where I coached a youth team and was on the committee. Wally is an Irishman who plays the bagpipes, and he was offering to play his pipes in the wedding. I accepted. He played wonderfully while everyone walked into the dining room at Plas Rhianfa, fair play to him.

The night before the wedding, the boys and I went to Talwrn to spend the night with Mam and Clive. The morning of 6 February was upon us very quickly; in less than a week Becky had managed to arrange a lovely wedding, and I was determined to put everything aside and enjoy our big day. I put on my suit and helped Siôn and Ianto do likewise. They were both really excited and fancied themselves no end in their suits and bow-ties.

When I arrived at Bangor Registry Office I remember thinking how nice the place looked, and how lovely it was to see everyone there. Mel, the photographer, had spent the morning at our house with Becky, her parents and Sarah, her bridesmaid, and he came into the registry office just before Becky arrived. While everyone was settling down in their seats he came up to me and said, 'She looks beautiful, mate, punching well above your weight.' I forgave him, seeing as he was absolutely spot on.

Steve, my stepbrother, had travelled from Brussels with his eldest son, Gruff, who was six at the time. Unfortunately his partner, Tracey, and their two other sons, Gwion and Osian, hadn't been able to come over because Gwion had chickenpox. Lois, Owen and Beca had come to the wedding with Steve, and although Lois was very nervous because she was reading in the service, she soon settled down and enjoyed the day with the others. The children were all looking forward to a day of fun with their cousins – Ffion and Elen, my stepbrother Andrew and his wife Sarah's girls; Luke and Holly, my brother Arwyn's children; and Erin, daughter of Gavin, my stepbrother on Dad's side.

I was really happy that James, the youngest of my stepbrothers, was coming to the wedding – although there was no sign of him in the registry office as the service was about to begin. James has been in the Marines since he was 19 years old and it's great to see him as he doesn't get much chance to come home. Incidentally, I realise my family is big and complicated, and I'll explain more about that later on.

Gary, the boys and I stepped out of the registry office to wait. After a while, Glenna, Becky's mum, and Sarah arrived in a vintage Rolls Royce, which was then going back to our house, about a mile away, to get Becky and Dylan, her stepfather. I went in, feeling a little bit nervous.

A few minutes later the music started playing, and Becky came in. Becky looks beautiful every day, but I'll never forget that feeling I got when I saw her in her wedding dress. I felt a chill down my spine and tears filled my eyes. I'd experienced the same feeling just after she gave birth to Siôn Arwyn – she wasn't wearing any makeup on that occasion and was totally exhausted, but at that moment she was the most beautiful vision I'd ever seen.

I managed to hold back the tears until Lois performed her reading. She was very emotional too, and had to pause a few seconds before being able to carry on. Of course, that was enough to start me crying too. Lois had done very well, and I was extremely proud of her. Siôn brought a smile to everyone's faces soon afterwards, as he'd been given the honour of carrying the rings in a 'special' box, and was taking his role very seriously!

There are spectacular views from Plas Rhianfa hotel in Anglesey across the Menai Straits and further to the mountains of Eryri. When we arrived there the bubbly was flowing and everyone was enjoying themselves. Plenty of photographs were taken (quite an undertaking, bearing in mind the complexity of my family) and we had enough time to socialise and relax before starting to eat. The food was wonderful and then it was time for the speeches. Dylan went first, and his speech started out fine. He made a joke of the fact that James, who has travelled the world with his job, hadn't managed to find the registry office until the end of the wedding, but it became increasingly difficult to make any sense of his words and he broke down and cried as he talked about Becky's dad, Dave, who died of cancer when Becky was fourteen. He was only 43 at the time, the same age as me when I got my diagnosis. I'd heard many people talk about Dave, who was a nurse lecturer, and no-one has a bad word to say about him. His death was obviously very hard for the entire family – he was a very talented man professionally and musically, and Siôn and Ianto will be very lucky if they get a small part of his talent.

It was my turn to speak next. Although I'd written my speech on cards – which included a few tales about Gary's and my escapades, words of thanks and a few words about Becky – unfortunately I'm sure nobody understood a word I said as I rambled on in tears! Things went from bad to worse, and Gary cried through his speech too. Looking at the wedding photos later, I noticed that Martin, the hotel manager, was crying buckets too as he listened to what we were saying!

Dad stepped in to save the day, eager to have his say. He's a good one for making people laugh, but I couldn't believe my ears when he said that Becky was the most beautiful bride he'd ever seen, bar one. He'd seen the first on 5 October 1968, according to him, namely Mam – the first of his three wives! Everyone laughed except Mam, but when the penny dropped she was laughing too.

We had a great day surrounded by family and friends, laughing and chatting. The wedding couldn't have gone any better if we'd had a year to arrange it.

Usually couples go on honeymoon, don't they – and a week or two in the Bahamas would have been lovely, but as I was starting my treatment it was impossible to arrange any kind of holiday. Despite that, I got a honeymoon that many men would absolutely love.

The day after the wedding we'd arranged to go to Dublin to watch Wales play rugby, and we enjoyed a fantastic weekend there with our friends Daf, Nia, Aled and Gwawr. We saw Dad there with his choir buddies (he sings in the Brythoniaid Male Voice Choir) and James was there with the Caernarfon Rugby Club boys. I forgot about everything for a few days, and although Wales got hammered by the Irish, a pint or two of Guinness and plenty of singing and laughter were a tremendous tonic.

This was our honeymoon!

꙳

Last night I had a dream about a box full of folded up pieces of paper. Each piece of paper had a word written on it. Everyone who knows Irfon had been asked to write one word that describes him and pop their paper in the box. The number of adjectives on the pieces of paper was overwhelming. I suppose that reflects the depth and richness of Irfon's personality. Words that recurred were 'strong' 'determined' and 'heroic'. I agree with all of them. I'm Irfon's best friend and that makes me special. I was allowed three pieces of paper not just one; two to describe Irfon and one to describe me. It's my dream so it's my prerogative. The words I chose to describe him reflect two of his characteristics that have underpinned our friendship from the first day I bumped in to him on Friday 21st October 1988, and which continue to form the cornerstone of our special friendship. They are the attributes that originally drew me towards him back then. They made me realise that he was somebody I'd be honoured to call my best friend, and that I'd thoroughly enjoy the experience too. The words remain as important to me today as they did then. The words on my two pieces of paper were 'funny' and 'honest'.

Irfon is without doubt one of the funniest people I've ever met. He has a natural wit and an ability to effortlessly weave this into everyday experiences. He has the foresight and the hindsight to find humour in almost every situation, especially those in which he is the butt of the joke. He has the gift of being able to laugh as much at himself as others do. His humour draws people in and, before they realise, they are part of the comedic drama unfolding around them. Even during sadder times when he could be forgiven for not feeling like laughing, he ignores convention and delivers some corkers. He even did this today, just after the palliative care team had visited him at home because he'd had a blip. He was in pain, he was nauseous and he was desperately tired, but we both cracked up at something he said in between dozing off. I've shed lots of tears with Irfon, most of them tears of laughter.

Irfon is shamelessly honest, saying it as it is. He always tells me the truth; even, no, *especially* when he thinks I might not like what I'll hear. He treats honesty as a duty to his best friend. You never lie to your best friend. We've never actually had that conversation; we never needed to. It's always just been a given. Our unwritten rule. If I need a plain honest answer, he's my go-to man.

My third piece of paper described me. It had written on it, in bold and underlined, the word 'honoured'. It best describes how I feel when I remind myself that I'm Irfon's best friend. It's how I feel when I think of the times we had, the experiences we shared and the security I feel when he's around. People associate me with Irfon. Immediately after they ask me how I am, they say 'and how's Irfon?'. It seems to come naturally to them. Like it's unthinkable that there could be one without the other. The pride this gives me is immeasurable.

Being older than Irfon, I assumed, when we met all those years ago, that I knew it all and could be a source of wise advice to my young mentee. How naive. I've learnt so much about life and living from him. How lucky I was to have bumped in to him that day.

Gary Porter Jones

Chapter 2

My Career

Before I go on to discuss my treatment, I'd like to say a few words about my career – mainly because I believe it helped me cope with the diagnosis.

I started my nursing career in February 1990. Mam took me to Ysbyty Gwynedd in Bangor late one Sunday afternoon, stopping at the porters' desk to pick up the key to my room in the nurses' home in the hospital grounds. Mam warned me to behave myself, work hard and so on, and I remember her saying that I'd probably have a room on a corridor with other men. I was really nervous.

There was no-one else about when we entered the building, Llys Miaren. My room was on the first floor, and there wasn't a sound there either when I arrived. Mam settled me in, made the bed and so on, and off she went. I was so nervous I stayed in my room until the next morning without coming out at all – I don't know why, because I was a very social person even in those days.

In the morning I needed to be at the hospital's School of Nursing by nine, so I woke up pretty early to make sure I'd be ready. I picked up my towel and walked down the corridor to the bathroom in my boxer shorts. The kitchen was at the same end of the corridor, and as I walked past I heard a voice call out 'hello'. In the kitchen were four girls in pyjamas, who gave me a friendly welcome. I walked on to the bathroom smiling like the cat that got the cream, certain now that I'd chosen the right career!

I became good friends with three of the girls who lived on the same corridor as me, and they became a big part of my life

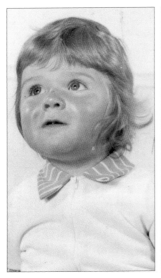

Nain was very annoyed that this photo didn't win the Bonny Baby competition she entered me into

Christmas 1977

Dad, Arwyn and me

Mam and me

Arwyn and I with Nain & Taid
Caernarfon and Max the dog

This is me: I called myself Gloria!

Christmas in Friars Avenue: (back) Nain Caernarfon, me, Taid
Caernarfon, (front) Taid Junction, my cousin Mandy, Uncle Gordon
and Arwyn

Ysgol y Garnedd primary school's folk dancing troupe, 1981

The Bangor Under 18 Rugby team, 1985-6 season.
I'm in the front row, second from left

Gary and myself

Dad and me

I loved being on the rugby field

Playing the euphonium in Beaumaris Brass Band

Andy, me, Robin, Tremayne and Alan, Butlin's, Pwllheli, 1985

Mam and me

Celebrating our engagement in Spain ... after our marriage!

On top of Snowdon, 24 June, 2016

One of the happiest days of my life

The dashing young nurse

Nurse of the Year, 2013

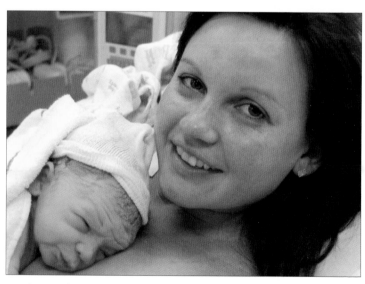

Becky stright after giving birth to Siôn Arwyn – I had never seen her look so beautiful

With Mr Malik and Claire in Aintree Hospital

Llanfair Hotshots and their proud coach

Me with Lois and Owen   *Friends for life!*

I grew a moustache for Movember 2013, not knowing I was ill

Welsh football stars Gareth Bale, Joe Ledley and Wayne Hennessey
supporting the cause

The message went far and wide

The Hawl i Fyw singers in the recording studio

Welsh singer and presenter
Elin Fflur

Meeting Carwyn Jones

With staff from Alaw Ward in our colourful wigs

After having my head shaved at the Urdd Eisteddfod

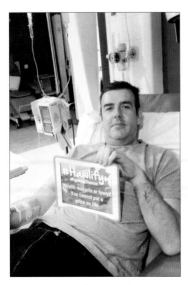

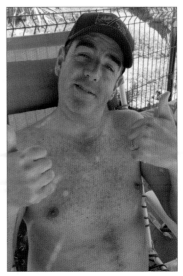

*Receiving the first dose of
Cetuximab at The Christie*

*The rash I developed after the
Cetuximab*

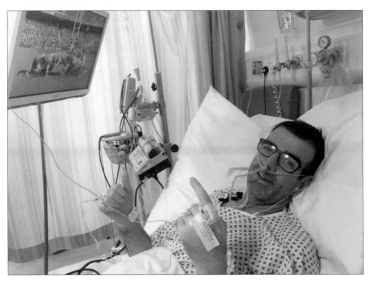

Watching the rugby after coming out of Intensive Care

Bangor's Santa Dash

I was made up: the letter from the Gorsedd of the Bards

The National Eisteddfod in Anglesey, 2017

Lois, Owen, Beca, Siôn and Ianto, 2014

during my nursing years. I'm still in touch with them today. Elen lived in the room next door to me; she was from Llandudno Junction and was quite a character. It wasn't unusual for her to come into my room in her pyjamas late at night, drunkenly singing and dancing around my bed while the other two fell about laughing behind her! In the room opposite me was Angela, an Irish girl who'd come to Bangor to train as a nurse. Angela was really kind, and invited me and two friends to stay at her house in Dublin during one international rugby weekend. I don't know what her parents thought of us as it was a very drunken few days! I'm sure they were terribly worried knowing that their darling daughter was going back to Wales accompanied by us three idiots! Doris from Talwrn completed the trio. She was a comedian too, but she was also the one who'd lay down the law when I left the kitchen or bathroom in a mess. I was spoiled, to tell the truth, as the three looked after me, and would sometimes feed me or iron a shirt for me if I was on my way out on a date. They were very quick to voice their opinions if any girl I invited home with me didn't come up to scratch!

Life in the nurses' home was great, and if I had my time all over again I'd follow exactly the same path. I made friends for life there, including Gary, who was on his third year of the nursing course when I was in the first. I'd met Gary before starting the course – he'd looked after me when I was on the orthopaedic ward following a rugby accident. He advised me to consider a career in nursing, suggesting strongly that it was something I would enjoy ... mainly because there were so many more female nurses than male! We were good mates, and mischievous to say the least!

Out of the two hundred people living in the nurses' home, only about ten percent were boys, and a percentage of those were gay, so there was plenty of choice for us. I had two or three ... or maybe more ... girlfriends during the three years, and I'm

Me in my student nurse's uniform

still friends with most of them to this day.

The hospital Social Club was a great place, but a bit too convenient, being some twenty yards from where we lived. Every Thursday night, in the early days, they held a disco, and usually there'd be a party in one of the doctors' rooms or on a nurses' corridor after that had ended. After a year or so, the disco was down to once a month, on payday, and on other nights people would just go there for a quiet pint. On Wednesday nights a group of us used to represent the club in the Bangor and District pool league, and we didn't do too badly!

My first three months in the nursing school passed by very quickly. By the second month the next group of students had arrived, including Nick, who became a good friend, and four other lads. There were more boys in that group than girls – unlucky, eh! Two months later another group started on their course, and there were no boys at all in that one! For a laugh, some of us decided to set up a welcoming club to make the students feel at home ... but mainly to assess which ones we fancied! Neil Madog, a hell of a case, took me up to the second floor of Llys Miaren to some young Irish girl's room to welcome her and invite her to join our trainspotters' group. The poor girl was very polite for about half an hour until she realised that we were pulling her leg. Luckily, she saw the funny side and joined us in the club for a pint that night.

The various characters in the nurses' accommodation were

good company. Neil used to play pranks on everyone, joined by his mate, Big Steve – and Nick was often the victim. One Thursday night, payday, Nick was working a late shift which meant that he wouldn't be back from work until after 9.30. In the meantime, Neil and Steve had emptied Nick's room, furniture and all, and laid everything out neatly in the car park. Of course, the fact that it was dark before Nick realised what had happened made the whole thing even funnier! Moving the furniture back was much more tricky as a pint or two had been consumed by then.

We were a big, fun-loving gang at that time. I had a lot of laughs with Emlyn, Janice Mercer and Lona – and a lad from Caernarfon known as 'Six', who lived unofficially with his girlfriend in the hall (a real character who spent far more time with the lads than with his girlfriend). I'm still in touch with them all, and each one has been in regular contact to see how I am since hearing about my illness. One of the girls, Karen O'Leary, works in The Christie Hospital in Manchester, and she used to come and see me when I was receiving treatment there.

Yes, I had a laugh during my course, but I was working hard on the wards too. In those days trainee nurses were an important part of the team on the wards – that's how we learnt, on the job, as it were. We all had to attend college every day for the first twelve weeks to learn the basics before being let loose on an orthopaedic ward for nine weeks. Learning how to make a bed, to wash and shave people and even how to talk to patients was an important part of that education.

My first ward required us to give injections to patients, and we were taught to do this by practising on oranges. I don't think it prepared us very well! Every morning one of the girls, usually Doris as she was the organised one, would wake us all up to make sure we were ready to walk up to the hospital on time. On Fridays getting up was harder because of the previous night's disco, but that barely affected our work in class or on

*Nick, Tony, Robbie, Gary, Paul, Alan and I at a barbecue
at my house in Hendrewen, Bangor*

the wards. There were eleven of us in the group, if I remember rightly, and only two of us were men: myself and a tall, bearded man named Boris. As it happened, Doris, Boris and I always used to sit together. I used to think I was quite the comedian when I introduced myself to external lecturers as Morris, after Doris and Boris had given their names!

As you might expect, we students were the target for some leg-pulling, especially in the early months. When I was on my first placement, one of the charge nurses sent me to one of the other wards to fetch a Fallopian tube. I repeated the term over and over under my breath in order to remember it, and couldn't understand why everyone was laughing – until I got down to the gynaecology ward and realised what the joke was! Sometimes, we'd get our own back. I remember a staff nurse on one ward, after losing one of the patients, asking one of my fellow students, 'Would you like to go into cubicle 4 to do last offices on Mr Jones?' He walked in and greeted the patient merrily with a 'Hello, Mr Jones, are you better?' The poor nurse's face was a picture!

During the second year, the lads (namely Neil, Nick, a lad called Peter Pay Day and myself) moved to a corridor together in Llys yr Onnen hall. Pete had been given that nickname due to his habit of spending all his money during the weekend after getting paid and going on a three-day binge of food and drink. He spent the rest of the month eating baked beans and everyone else's leftovers! Gary was more sensible, and he stayed at Llys y Fedwen. We were a nightmare for the accommodation officer, and we could have been chucked out on more than one occasion had we been caught. We weren't allowed pets of any kind in the nurses' home, but Neil had a dog called Fletch there, one he'd found in the hospital, and a cat called Mozart that he'd saved from a box on the roadside in Dwygyfylchi. Girlfriends stayed over quite often and things sometimes got messy, especially if we decided to hold a party on a Thursday night.

I loved the high jinks of those days – but I also adored nursing as a job. Every ward I worked on was a pleasure, and I was getting excellent reports. I started the second year with nine weeks in the dermatology department, and a friend named Angela was placed on the same ward. The manager was Sister Bentley, and she was a pleasure to work with, as she seemed to favour and praise me. Angela was working just as hard as I was, of course, so she wasn't at all happy when I got higher marks than her and a glowing report from Sister Bentley. I was placed in theatre for a while, then I had a period at Bryn y Neuadd Hospital caring for people with learning disabilities. I loved it there too, and started to think that I'd like to carry on with that kind of work during my career.

At the end of the second year each of us had to do three months of night shifts. My mentor on Ogwen ward was called Bethan, and she was very good with me although she quickly learnt that night shifts didn't suit me. I often found it difficult to stay awake. But one of the other nurses on the ward didn't like me at all. I didn't really agree with her way of doing some things, and I didn't think much of her methods which were, in my opinion, old-fashioned. I realise now that she was a very experienced nurse, and had I shown more patience I would have learnt a lot from her. Bethan has cared for me on Ogwen ward recently, on night shifts. I don't know how she copes with night work, but she's a brilliant nurse.

The third year came quickly and we were expected to grow up and settle down a bit. Exams were getting harder and there was more work to be done. By then the nursing education structure had changed and we were now Bangor University students, and although we got to finish our original course the new curriculum had influenced our lecturers and the focus became more academic. On the wards we were expected to take more responsibility, and everyone was starting to think about jobs.

In that third year I was placed on the children's ward, which was the best placement I had throughout my training. I loved it there, and was in my element with the patients and parents as well as the staff. Sister Rosser, the unit manager, hadn't been keen for men to work there and some of the staff felt that her attitude was old-fashioned – she didn't believe it was appropriate for men to look after children. Nevertheless, I got on well with her, and at the end of the placement I was called into her office. She asked me if I was interested in working there after registering, a few months later. Of course, I was over the moon. I waited for a call to arrange an interview – but it turned out that the informal chat in her office *was* the interview, and the paperwork was ready for me when I learnt that I'd been successful and passed the course. Obviously that was more acceptable in those days, as ward nurses got to know the students during their placements and by word of mouth (finding out how good, or how clueless, they were).

By April 1993 I'd started working on the children's ward and was learning fast. I was really enjoying my work and very happy to be working there, as I got to spend some time working alongside experienced nurses who influenced me enormously. Following the terrible story of Beverley Allitt, the nurse who murdered several children in an English hospital, UK-wide legislation was changed: all nurses working on children's wards were required to qualify as dedicated children's nurses. Of course, I was a general registered nurse, just like today's adult nurses, which meant that I'd have no chance of advancing my career in paediatric nursing unless I was re-trained. I started to feel frustrated and impatient. Sister Rosser arranged to send all nurses in my situation on secondment to train as children's nurses, but as I was one of the newest arrivals it would be years before my turn came around. Even so, I decided that as I was enjoying my work so much I'd stay there and wait patiently for a few years.

A few weeks later I was walking along one of the hospital corridors on my way to the canteen for lunch. One of the ward nurses came to meet me, in tears because a member of her family was ill. I sat down with her to talk, and she told me that she wouldn't be able to attend the children's nursing course that she was due to embark on in a fortnight. She suggested that I should take her place. Without wasting a second, I went straight to the nursing director's office. Luckily, she agreed to see me, and I explained the situation – and she agreed to support my application as long as the head nurses consented. Unfortunately, Sister Rosser was away for a while and Sister Kath was standing in. I had a very good relationship with her, and we had a lot of fun working together, however there was no guarantee that my application would be supported, with so many of the other nurses also waiting to be accepted. I gave Sister Kath a big kiss when she agreed to the request, and off I went to book a place on the course in Liverpool. The course organiser was more than happy for me to fill the vacancy, so in September 1994 I set off to Liverpool to train as a children's nurse.

Living up in Liverpool from Monday to Friday, although a bit stressful at times, was a fantastic experience. However, in the meantime I'd started a relationship with a girl called Lisa who was, by that time, pregnant. I'll tell you more about this later, but the baby was due that November – so I had to be ready to travel back at short notice when the baby was on the way! As luck would have it, I was at home when Lois arrived in December, and working locally too, conveniently, so I was able to spend quite a lot of time with her in those early days.

I was mainly placed in Alder Hey Hospital in Liverpool, and working on the wards and in casualty there was a great experience, allowing me to see some very interesting cases come and go. I loved the Scousers' sense of humour – and as the name 'Irfon' isn't very easy to pronounce I had a lot of laughs with the patients, parents and, of course, nurses who called me something different every day! I remember the head nurse on ward C3 coming to me in a fit of giggles one day – one of the mothers had turned to her and said, 'That Russian fella's a bit of alright isn't he?'. While treating one boy's leg in casualty, I remember noticing that the father was staring at my name badge (I had one official badge and another with 'Irfon' written on a sheep's back ... which was perhaps a clue to my nationality). After a while he asked, 'Are you Swedish?'.

Most were fully aware that I was Welsh, and this was sometimes an advantage. Once, I was moved from one ward to another to attend to a very young Welsh boy who didn't understand English. It felt good to be able to help that little boy and make his time in hospital easier. Shortly after I started talking publicly about my illness, I received a message from his mother reminding me of that time, and thanking me for making a big difference to him and his family. Many ex-patients have contacted me since I've been ill – all the messages I've received give me great pleasure, though I sometimes end up in tears reading them.

Since starting in the field of children's nursing I'd been very interested in the psychological aspect. I was attracted to such cases, and during my training I spent a brief period in the psychiatric unit at Alder Hey, and a longer period at Gwynfa in Colwyn Bay, which was a residential unit for young people from north Wales with severe mental health problems. While I was there I met a senior nurse called Steve Riley, who made quite an impression on me, and I felt strongly that this was the route I wanted to follow.

By January 1996 I was back on Ysbyty Gwynedd children's ward and almost immediately I was promoted to a higher grade. Life was good, and we had a lot of laughs there. At times, I'd walk around the ward with medicine pots on my eyes, a bed pan on my head and my trousers pulled up to my chest to raise the children's spirits! They loved it, of course, and I remember many a parent saying that all the tomfoolery made their children's time in hospital much easier. Of course, I needed to be sensible too, and there were a few very sad periods on the ward, especially if a patient died. That always affected me deeply, but it was also important to carry on for the sake of the other patients. It helped that we were a very close team and were all supportive of each other when any one of us was upset.

I continued to be drawn towards cases involving psychiatric problems. When psychiatrists visited the ward to assess a patient I was always eager to observe these assessments, and I learnt a great deal from Dr Lynch and Dr Wilkinson. I couldn't believe my luck when an opportunity arose to apply for a job in the Child and Adolescent Mental Health Service (CAMHS), a job that included training for the first year. The job title was

Child Therapist, and I underwent the hardest interview ever by two psychiatrists and two psychologists – it felt more like an assessment of my own mental health than an interview! No-one expected me to be successful as I didn't have much experience in the area, but I felt quietly confident, believing that my experience of working with children and families in Bangor and Liverpool was a good grounding. On the day of the interview I was working on the ward, and had taken time off to attend it. Later that afternoon I was back at work on the ward when a phone call came from Dr Jean Lyon, CAMHS manager and psychologist, offering me the job. I immediately and delightedly accepted.

In September 1997 I started in my post as Child Therapist, and it was obvious that I had a lot to learn. By now Lisa and I had bought our first house in Llanfairpwll and Lois was two years old. Although nervous (I was only 27, and the closest in age to me on the team was 40) I was very enthusiastic in embarking on my new journey as a therapist. The team was small and I was given a large office to share with Mari, a very experienced social worker. Mari and I were the only two Welsh-speaking therapists, and very soon, as I developed skills and confidence, I was the one who saw many of the children for whom a Welsh speaker had been requested. I was in a particularly privileged position, as the staff were all keen to share their knowledge and skills with me. I'd spend one day with Dr Lynch in the Meirionnydd and South Arfon area, and another day with Dr Wilkinson in Ynys Môn and North Arfon. The rest of my time was spent in the company of Dr Lyon or Dr Judy Hutchings, vastly experienced psychologists. I was sent on numerous training courses, and in the first year I was very happy to return to Alder Hey on a family therapy course.

In CAMHS, not one day went by without my sharing a joke and a laugh with the secretaries – Manon and Elaine to begin with, then Helen, Maggi and Sandy. I was gradually getting to understand more and more, and my confidence was growing from year to year. In 2001, following the Welsh Government's publication of a new strategy entitled 'Everybody's Business', I was appointed to the new post of Primary Care Specialist. My principal role was early intervention, working closely with GPs, schools, health visitors etc., offering them support and training. In 2002 I was asked by Alun Davies, Director of Mental Health Services, whether I'd be interested in applying to spend time in Pennsylvania and New York on an exchange and study programme arranged by Rotary International.

After a series of meetings, presentations and interviews I was chosen to go as one of five, and we had to meet regularly for six months before flying to America. The leader was Keith, a retired GP from Heswall, and the three others I'd be spending time in their company were a solicitor from Wallasey named Louise, Christine who was a Communications Officer in Manchester, and Andy, a forestry manager from Denbigh. During my time in the States, I spent a happy period working in schools, teaching the pupils about Wales and teaching them how to cope with the World Trade Centre disaster which had happened the year before. I got to visit children's residential homes, mental health services, hospitals and social services, and as well as working I had to give presentations in conferences and meetings, as did the others.

The rest of our time was free for socialising. As the only Welsh speaker I was treated like a king – the Welsh are highly regarded in the States because of our part in developing the quarries there in the 18th century. I recited the Lord's Prayer in a jam-packed Welsh church, and attended an eisteddfod (and ate twice my weight in Welsh cakes, or 'Welsh cookies' as they're known there).

Although the trip was a wonderful experience which developed my skills and confidence, six weeks was a long time to spend so far away from my family. I hadn't left the children before – Owen and Beca were born by then, and Beca had walked for the first time while I was away. I felt really homesick, and Lois, who was then about seven years old, had found it very hard to cope with my absence too. I sent daily e-mails to my family, and she'd send back a little story about whatever she'd been doing that day. One day, she typed out the words of the Welsh hymn 'Dwy Law yn Erfyn' so that I could practise singing it, for us to sing it together after I got home. Bless her!

I was still enjoying my work in CAMHS and was having more say in service management decisions. The team was growing slowly, but I was keen to develop the early intervention and nursing element. In 2003 an opportunity arose to apply for a senior nurse post with responsibility for developing a nursing service in CAMHS – but unfortunately, although CAMHS was a children's service, the national guidelines in the field had changed. CAMHS nurses now had to be qualified as mental health nurses, which meant that I couldn't apply. Looking into it, I discovered that similar rules existed for registered nurses working with the elderly mentally ill. Luckily, the university and government had agreed to provide a one-year course for nurses with experience in the field to enable them to qualify as mental health nurses. It was a very intensive course and I spent much of 2004 attending lectures, on placement with the adult mental health services and in front of a computer late at night writing essays! Although I protested at the time about having to do the course, I have to confess that the experience was valuable, making me a better nurse and therapist as a result. In 2005 I was promoted to the post of senior nurse – despite being the only nurse in the service!

I then set about writing papers and requests for a team of nurses and early intervention workers, and by 2008 I'd been promoted to become head of the service. Many of the old faces had now gone and a young, enthusiastic team was in place – about half of them Welsh speakers. Many of the team members were keen to develop the service with me and I was given tremendous support by most of them.

Outside work, too, major changes had happened in my life. I'd had to give up playing rugby because my knee was knackered – but at 36 years old, I was one of the team's veterans so maybe it was time for me to give it up anyway. Lisa and I had separated and I was in a relationship with Becky, but I enjoyed spending time with the children as often as I could, and helped coach Owen's football team. Lois took up playing the trumpet at school and that pleased me enormously as I'd been a trumpet player myself until I was 16, when rugby took over. But one day, as I was taking Lois to Beaumaris Band rehearsals, Gwyn Evans, the conductor, asked me what I was doing there without an instrument! Before I could turn around I had an euphonium in my hand and had joined Beaumaris Youth Band! Lois gave up the trumpet, unfortunately, but I carried on playing until I became ill (albeit not in the youth band!).

In 2010 the Welsh NHS boards were restructured and Betsi Cadwaladr Health Board was created to serve North Wales. CAMHS was located in the children's department, and soon all service managers received a letter explaining that our positions were in jeopardy and that we would be required to apply for posts in the new structure. The manager at that time was Yvonne Harding, who managed to allay our fears. She was in charge of a team of about ten service managers across the north, and each of us got a post. My responsibility from then on was running CAMHS and the Môn and Gwynedd child disability services.

I didn't have much experience of working in the field of child disability, and I'm conscious that this affected my ability to manage some elements of the service, as some people lacked confidence in my competence. The service was a partnership with Social Services, but the fact that two counties, Môn and

Gwynedd, were being served complicated matters to some extent as I had to deal with different individuals in the two areas. In Gwynedd progress was slightly quicker despite a serious lack of resources in a period of cutbacks. Iona Griffiths was the Gwynedd manager – she totally understood the needs of service users, and when I received my diagnosis Iona and the Gwynedd service staff were really kind towards me.

I worked most closely with the nursing team, of course. Some of them were very experienced and coping well, considering the serious pressure on such a small team. Two of those nurses were Meinir and Fiona, working in Anglesey. When the time came for me to leave, Meinir organised a dinner for me with the entire team, and she's kept in touch ever since.

After about two years Yvonne decided to change the structure – instead of managing the disability services, I was to take a leading part in CAMHS across north Wales. That entailed a lot more travelling, and as we had to use Health Board cars I spent hours in a grey Fiesta going up and down the A55. I spent a great deal of time in Wrexham and Flintshire – services there were very different to what I'd been accustomed to in the west. I was keen to make changes and I gained the support of most of the team members there to do that. Of course, it wasn't easy – not everyone likes change, and I had to discuss everything in detail with other outside agency managers such as social services, education and the voluntary and charitable sector. I was now spending more and more time in meetings, with no contact at all with patients. Although I was on quite a good salary due to my managerial role, I sometimes regretted climbing the career ladder. Working with children and young people was what made me happy – that was where my skills lay, and that's what I was trained for. The travelling was stressful as I'd leave the house at seven thirty in the morning sometimes and not get home until six or seven at night.

I learnt a great deal over the years in CAMHS, and I've used those skills in my personal life. My attitude towards life has always been positive, but I believe strongly that working with people less fortunate than myself, people who have shown such strength and resilience, has made me very grateful for what I've got. Some family members sometimes suspect that I use my therapy skills unfairly – during a row, for example – but that would never work with Becky! I'm really grateful to have enjoyed a very successful career – not many people can say that they'd make the same choices if they could live their lives again, but I'd choose to be a nurse every time.

The early years of my career provided me with a great grounding, which enabled me to be professional throughout my career. The one thing I never considered, of course, was how I'd cope if I were ever a patient, and having to experience a nurse's life from the other side.

෨෧

When I think of Irfon at work a smile spreads across my face: not because he was the first nurse in the Gwynedd and Anglesey Child Guidance team, nor because he was appointed to the role of Child and Adolescent Mental Health Service (CAMHS) Manager some twenty years later. It's because Irfon always brought fun, humour and care to a field of work which can be heavy and, at times, sad.

Irfon could always light up a boring meeting with a smile and a laugh, very often when those involved least expected it. It didn't matter whether it was a meeting just between the service staff or a regional meeting of high-ranking managers, it wouldn't pass without a light moment instigated by Irfon. He could also raise his colleagues' spirits with mischievous scams such as the HBS (Hot Beverage Society) which would meet on a monthly basis to discuss the importance of hot drinks in the workplace and the best biscuits to accompany them, following the 'NICE biscuit guidelines', obviously!

Behind the smile and the japes there was genuine concern for his colleagues, especially after he was promoted to Service Manager. Irfon may not have been the best at collecting staff timesheets and so on, but he excelled at keeping in contact with every member of staff to ensure they were OK. After arriving back from important meetings which could be held anywhere across the North Wales region, Irfon would return to Talafon (the Gwynedd and Anglesey CAMHS office) and spend time chatting to the staff – from the cleaning lady to the most experienced psychiatrist – to make sure they were coping well in work. The sound of laughter was very often heard from the offices Irfon visited.

But there's another reason why I always smile when I think of Irfon's attitude in work – his focus was always on the children and the young people, the users of the service, and their families. Mental health (the emphasis being on the health) was very close to his heart, as it still is. Irfon was the first person I heard talking regularly about reducing the stigma attached to mental health, and he went on to develop the 'Mental Health Matters' programme for secondary school pupils, a programme to break down the stigma associated with mental health and one which encouraged young people to talk to a familiar adult if they felt that their emotions were getting on top of them. Irfon was well ahead of his time: this is exactly what much later on the Welsh Assembly Government introduced with their 'Talk To Me' suicide prevention initiative, encouraging people to talk about their feelings as this significantly decreased the number of suicides. He went on to win a Royal College of Nursing prize, the Welsh Children's Nurse of the year award for this work, and he, along with a number of his colleagues, also won a Betsi Cadwaladr University Health Board award for their work in schools.

Unfortunately, Irfon had to take early retirement, and I still miss him. I miss the way he prioritised every individual who came into contact with the service, miss his care for those individuals and for each and every member of staff, miss his fun and laughter and his big heart.

Dr Gwenllian Parry, Consultant Clinical Psychiatrist
Gwynedd and Anglesey Child and Adolescent
Mental Health Service

Chapter 3

Resilience

Resilience is a word I've used a lot over the last few years. While working for the children and young people's mental health service I was interested in early intervention, and strongly believed in the value of discussing mental health issues openly with children, young people and adults. A stigma still exists about mental health and to this day I'm eager to work on reducing this stigma.

Working in the field of mental health has made me think more about my own personality. Why have I turned out as I have? Was I born like this or has my upbringing influenced who I am today? Since my diagnosis people have often asked how I've kept so positive and strong all the time. Of course, we can't change the past, but I've thought a lot about my own background, my upbringing and my relationship with family and friends, and I'm certain that my past has enormously influenced my life and ability to cope ... that is, my resilience.

To this day, I can't understand how on earth Mam and Dad came to be together. They're like chalk and cheese, and I can't think of a single thing they have in common – other than being parents to Arwyn and myself! I've had a few chats with Mam about this, and she explained that Dad was a real hunk when he was young: popular, a real character and a bit of a charmer. Mam was a very pretty young girl too and was obviously vivacious, and I'm sure she was a feather in Dad's cap when they started going out together. They were both in the police force – Mam, Eirlys, originally from Llandudno Junction, was a policewoman in Holyhead and Dad, Bryan, from Caernarfon,

My parents in their uniforms

was a policeman in Cemaes Bay – when they met, and before long they were married. I was born in 1970; by then, Mam had finished in the police force and Dad was a policeman in Bangor. We lived in Friars Avenue in Hirael, Bangor. Two years later my brother, Arwyn, was born.

In the seventies and eighties it was usual for policemen to be moved from area to area to work, and in 1973 Dad was transferred to Colwyn Bay. We lived behind the fire station there, and I remember the firemen throwing ice creams through the window into our back garden where Arwyn and I were playing. But we weren't there long before Dad was transferred to Blaenau Ffestiniog. By that time I was four years old, and I have hazy memories of events there. We lived in Wynne Road, at the bottom of the hill next door to a chapel, and on the square where there was quite a good park. I remember going to nursery school, learning to ride a bike – and once, I saw a sheep enter the house! Dad was a member of the

Me with my parents
around 1971

Brythoniaid Male Voice Choir there and he sometimes used to take me with him to choir practice.

Very soon Dad was moved again, and by the time I was five years old I lived in Pen-y-groes. I remember our time there well, and though we were only there two years, I have very fond memories of the place, and am still in touch with some of my old friends. That's where I have my first memory of being in school – I don't remember much about the classes but I do remember playing on the yard, and for some reason I can remember running around wildly shouting 'Who wants to play Batman and Robin? Who wants to play Batman and Robin?' with the other boys. Anyone who wanted to play would join the line and start running with us until the bell rang. To this day, I can't remember what the Batman and Robin game was!

It was in Pen-y-groes that I was introduced to football for the first time, by Aled Griffiths and Aled Jones. Aled Jones supported Leeds United and Aled Griffiths was a Liverpool fan. I had my first experience of watching a live game with Aled Griffiths and his father, and I was really excited on the bus on the way to Liverpool to see the Reds play Ipswich. When we arrived there, we were told the bad news – the match was postponed due to a frozen pitch! Even so, I remember the trip well, and the delicious plate of fish and chips I enjoyed that day. It's hard to believe that we only lived there for two years, and when I see the two Aleds from time to time we talk about the old days as if I'd been there for years and years.

Quite a lot of children lived in our street in Hen Lôn, and I remember Arwyn going into one of the back gardens, having been attracted to a rope swing that was hanging from the branch of a tree. Unfortunately, it wasn't a swing but a trap that someone had left there. Within seconds of touching the rope a pretty big rock came down from the tree and struck Arwyn on his head. There was blood everywhere and he was rushed to the doctor to have the wound stitched up. A few weeks later Arwyn started to lose weight, and complained of being terribly thirsty. Mam took him to see the doctor and he was sent straight to St David's Hospital where tests confirmed that he was suffering from diabetes.

The family moved back to Bangor after two years, and I remember feeling awfully sad about leaving Pen-y-groes, and telling Mam and Dad that I'd never be able to make new friends and that I didn't want to go to another school. I sometimes

Arwyn and I in Colwyn Bay fire station around 1974

wonder what effect this had on me, but I've concluded that having to make new friends and say goodbye to old ones has had a positive influence on me. To this day, I find it easy to communicate and get to know new people.

Because of the diabetes, Arwyn spent quite a lot of time in hospital as a child, in Bangor and at Alder Hey, Liverpool. I took a great interest in his illness, and tried to find out everything about the condition. We were both very close, and I used to really miss him when he was in hospital. On their regular visits to the children's clinic at St. David's Hospital, Mam and Arwyn encountered other families who were in the same boat. With the assistance of some of these, such as Di Barnes from Bangor and Rhiannon from Rhosybol, Mam set up the Gwynedd and Môn diabetes support group. Rhiannon had three boys, Gwyndaf, Osian and Aneurin, and we became friends, and had loads of fun on trips to places like the Sun Centre swimming complex in Rhyl.

Arwyn was diagnosed with diabetes shortly after this photo was taken in Pen-y-groes primary school

Of course, it wasn't just Arwyn that I missed. Mam usually stayed with him in hospital, and Dad and I would visit when Dad wasn't working. While Dad was at work, Nain Caernarfon looked after me mostly, and I enjoyed spending time at their home, Valetta, in Cae Mur, Caernarfon. Occasionally, I've worn my professional hat and tried to analyse what influence that situation had on me, when I was between seven and nine years old, but I haven't managed to work it out.

Although I missed Mam and Arwyn, having my grandmother

One of my birthday parties in Pen-y-groes

look after me was great. I was very close to Nain and respected her enormously – she was a strong, independent and very kind woman who loved being in the kitchen, and I loved eating her food! Taid spent a lot of time with us too. He was Dad's stepfather, as his father had died when he was two years old and Nain had remarried when Dad was six. I have very happy memories of gardening in Taid's plot in Caernarfon and spending hours in fields picking blackberries, really looking forward to the tart that Nain would bake for tea.

As I grew older, I continued to visit them regularly for tea and a chat. Taid had been a quarryman all his life, and his health had suffered due to his career. For years he used a nebuliser to help his breathing ... but he'd stop halfway through the treatment for a smoke! Shortly afterwards he was on regular oxygen through a tube in his nose, and I very often held my breath watching him light a cigarette in case he blew up the house! I was about eighteen by then, and Nain was in a wheelchair, unable to walk at all, and despite his own health problems Taid looked after her until he died. Nain had to go into a home after that, and I promised to carry on visiting her every week. Sometimes I'd take her out shopping for the day to Bangor or Llandudno in the car – she loved going and insisted on buying us a big lunch in a café. When Lois was little she came with us occasionally, but pushing the wheelchair with Nain in it and Lois sitting on her knee was a bit tricky. Nain's death was a great loss, but I'm sure she would take great pleasure in realising how much she influenced me. I feel very privileged to have spent so much time with her over the years.

Another member of Dad's family I was close to was Auntie May, my great grandfather's sister and a real character. She also lived in Caernarfon and I visited her regularly too, enjoying a cup of tea while she had a glass of sherry! I remember Auntie May as a woman who was always full of fun and it was always a pleasure to see her.

I have fond memories of my two great grandmothers and a great grandfather on Mam's side of the family – Mam's grandparents, Nan Nan and Deidi, lived with Nain and Taid in Llandudno Junction. Mam was very close to Nan Nan and Deidi, and they were delighted when I was born. Nan Nan died when I was two years old but even so I have a recollection of her feeding porridge to Shandy, the white poodle, and scolding Deidi for not getting out of bed! Deidi spent hours with Arwyn and I playing soldiers, and I'd follow him around the house marching and shouting like an army sergeant. Deidi died on his eightieth birthday in 1980. I was ten at the time, and this was my first real experience of loss. For some reason I didn't go to his funeral – I don't know whether by choice or not. I believe strongly in letting children attend the funeral after losing someone close to them as it's an important part of the grieving process, but in those days I'm sure Nain and Taid would have said that a funeral was no place for children.

Four generations: Nan Nan, Nain Junction, Mam and me

Arwyn and I with Aunty May and Max, the dog

I believe strongly that people who have the chance to enjoy relationships with their grandparents are very lucky – I was allowed that privilege and the boys, Siôn and Ianto, visit their great grandparents as well.

In November 1980 Mam, Arwyn and I had taken Nain back home to Llandudno Junction – she'd been staying with us while Taid was on a trip with his choir, Côr y Maelgwn, in America. During our journey home in our blue Datsun, it was raining heavily. Mam was driving, I was lying on the back seat because I got carsick and Arwyn was sat in the back with me. Within seconds of reaching Conwy bridge we had a horrendous accident. Mam had skidded on a puddle and the car had hit another car on the other side of the road. Mam was thrown through the windscreen and Arwyn was unconscious. There were no rear doors so I pushed Mam's seat forward and climbed out. I looked at Mam – she'd injured her eye and was obviously in serious pain – and I ran to the car we'd collided with. Blood was pouring down the face of the man in that car too. Someone held and comforted me, and Arwyn and I were placed to sit on a wall, and a blanket wrapped around us. The ambulance drove away without Arwyn and myself (I don't know whether this was intentional), but luckily a family who knew Mam and Dad were a few cars behind us: John and Sonia Thompson from Bangor. They were on their way home with four boys in the back of the car, including their son, Tremayne, who became a firm friend of mine in my teens. They took us back to Llandudno Junction and let Nain and Taid know what had happened. Taid stayed in the house with the four boys and Nain accompanied us to Llandudno Hospital where the ambulance had taken Mam.

Meanwhile, Dad was at work in Bangor when he received the news about the accident. When he got to Conwy and saw the car he thought for sure that we'd all been killed, but when he discovered that Arwyn and I were together on the children's ward he rushed there and spent all night pacing up and down the corridor. I had internal bleeding and Arwyn had suffered a blow to his jaw, and the sugar levels in his body went haywire for a while. We were both in hospital for about a fortnight. I remember having a hell of a shock when Dad brought Mam down to the children's ward in a wheelchair to see us – she had a big bandage around her swollen head and dried blood all over her face. I didn't know at the time, of course, how ill she was. As it turned out, she was lucky to be alive. She had hundreds of stitches in her head, and she'd broken her knee and numerous ribs. Mam looks exceptionally good today considering what happened to her, but she received various treatments for years following that accident. To this day she has trouble closing her eyes to go to sleep, and little fragments of glass emerge from her forehead every now and then too, even after nearly forty years.

Ysgol y Garnedd football team

Following that accident I remember going through a period of feeling very sorry for myself. I was tearful, suffered terrible nightmares and I relived parts of the accident. If I were a child today, I'd probably have been diagnosed with PTSD (Post Traumatic Stress Disorder). Mam had to gently encourage me to put it all behind me and try and forget about it, and after that things started to get better.

When the accident happened, I was in my last year at primary school, Ysgol y Garnedd, Bangor, and my teachers and friends were a great comfort to me. I remember being delighted when I received a giant card signed by all the children in the class and a little letter from each of them.

By this time sports had become an important part of my life. I played football whenever I could, and was captain of the school football team (thinking I was the bee's knees!). I also loved taking part in the school sports day, but had to get used to

Me, Robin Jones (Llanfairfechan), Robin McBryde and Mark Baines

coming second to my friend Alan Owen in those sports – which is how it remained for years!

After very happy years in Ysgol y Garnedd, the idea of going to secondary school, Ysgol Tryfan, scared me. I needn't have worried – in no time at all I'd settled down and made new friends like Berwyn from Llanfairfechan. Berwyn, Alan Owen and I were thick as thieves, meeting at weekends in each other's homes.

Growing up in Hirael was great – there were plenty of children living in the area and enough lads playing football in the field by the swimming pool every weekend in winter and every day and evening during the summer. Big gangs of us used to play 'tigers and hunters' – one group, the tigers, would go and hide, and the other group would hunt them. The game's boundaries were wide and you could go as far as the bottom of town, the pier in Garth and the Roman Camp in Upper Garth. It could take all day to find everyone, and it was sometimes easier to give up and go home when teatime came rather than finish the game!

Alan and I were selected for the Ysgol Tryfan football team, but the P.E. teacher, Mr Richie Haines, preferred rugby to football. By the time I reached the second year he'd persuaded me to take up rugby, and I was transferred to the school team along with Alan Owen (who else?), who was a great player. My interest in rugby grew and the obsession with football disappeared very quickly, given that I'd started playing basketball too. I see Mr Haines from time to time, and he told me recently that he thought I was a very good basketball player, far better than my rugby. I wasn't sure how to take that! Another boy who played rugby and basketball with me was Robin McBryde, and that's when our friendship developed.

Of course, sport wasn't the only purpose of school, although that was my main focus. I looked back at my school reports recently – the first three years were excellent, with

Good times!

I had saved up some of my own money to buy this bike, and I thought the world of it

quite a good report in all subjects. By form four, the comment for every subject, apart from music and P.E., was 'can do better'.

I used Mam and Dad's marriage breakdown as an excuse for the deterioration in my educational development. When they announced that they were separating, Arwyn and I were devastated. Arwyn tried for weeks to persuade them to get back together, but I wanted to forget everything, and spent as much time as possible with my friends. Mam went to live with Nain and Taid in Llandudno Junction and Dad stayed at our home in Bangor; I was allowed to choose who I wanted to live with, and I chose to stay with Dad in Bangor. I'm aware that Mam has spent years worrying about this, and looking back I'm sure I would have done much better in school under Mam's supervision. Dad did nothing wrong, of course, but he didn't attach as much importance to the academic side as Mam. Arwyn chose to live with Mam, but in reality we were both able to come and go to both their houses as Mam and Dad dealt with things really well – they used to attend school activities or parents' evenings together, and discussed issues involving Arwyn and I regularly.

During that uncertain period, my friends became very important to me. By then Alan, Robin and I had joined Bangor Rugby Club, where Tremayne was a member too (it was his family that helped us on the night of the car accident) and the four of us became friends. A lad named Andy Williams became one of the gang as well – Andy didn't play rugby but he was a brilliant cricketer, and during the summer that's what Alan, Robin and I did too.

As well as our interest in sport, Robin and I were members of the Menai Bridge Brass Band, him on the bass trombone and myself on the euphonium. Unfortunately, I sat in front of Robin in the rehearsals and sometimes his trombone slide would hit my backside in the middle of a piece of music! Spending time with Alan, Robin, Tremayne and Andy was a great comfort to

With Nain and Taid Caernarfon on my cousin Mandy's wedding day

me after Mam and Dad's separation. We'd walk up and down the high street in Bangor – it was a busy street in those days – and when we had money we'd go for a cup of tea to the Penguin Café. Sometimes we'd hang out in my bedroom, playing darts, listening to pop music, talking about girls and putting the world to rights. Of course, weekends were filled with rugby or cricket, and on Sundays there'd be frequent rugby matches in Manchester, the Wirral and around Chester. We'd have a good time on the buses on the way home, singing inappropriate songs, playing cards and chatting.

Life was good, although I still felt sad about the situation at home. After a while, when I was about 14, Dad's girlfriend, Helen, and her two sons, Gavin who was six and James who was eighteen months old, came to live with us. I very soon developed a close relationship with the boys, and I really enjoyed spending time and playing with them, or babysitting when Dad and Helen went out. But things in Bangor didn't remain stable for very long, either, as Dad and Helen used to fight, leaving me to try and comfort the little boys in the midst of the shouting. Dad had retired from the police by then and he decided to follow his dream of running a pub. When he told Arwyn and I that he'd got an opportunity to run the Morgan Lloyd on the Maes in Caernarfon we were both upset. No way was I going to live in Caernarfon – as a Bangor lad, I'd be asking for trouble! At the time there was bad blood between Bangor

With Taid Junction in the caravan in Conwy

Arwyn and I in Friars Avenue, Bangor

Nan Nan and Deidi

Andrew, Steven, Arwyn and myself on Mam and Clive's wedding day

and Caernarfon youths, and always some kind of vendetta between the two town's gangs. As it turned out, we didn't move from Bangor until I was 16, although Dad and Helen took over the Morgan Lloyd a few years prior to that.

My O-level results were very disappointing. In all honesty, I didn't revise at all for the exams, and didn't care about them either. I was working by then at the Morgan Lloyd and enjoying life between that and the rugby.

Nevertheless, I decided to enrol at Bangor Technical College, regarding it as a second chance. The course was interesting at times, and I must have matured to some extent as by that time I was ready to work and wanted to pass the GCSE exams. During the course, I got injured in a rugby game and spent time at Walton hospital in Liverpool and Ysbyty Gwynedd – an experience that made me decide that nursing was the career for me. After two years in college I managed to pass, and got adequate qualifications to start a nursing career.

I was still working at the Morgan Lloyd and going to stay with Mam regularly. By then she'd married my stepfather, Clive, and they'd moved to Menai Bridge with Arwyn along with Clive's two sons, Andrew and Steven. From the minute I met Clive, I knew we'd get on well. He was a massive rugby fan, and of course, being a native of Carmarthenshire, he was a proud Scarlet. We both used to debate who were the best players and teams and so on, and he took us regularly to watch Llanelli play, as the team tended to reach the Welsh Cup final nearly every year. His mother, Nanna Cacan, lived in Glangwili, and that's where we stayed when we went to watch the rugby.

The fact that Mam and Clive had moved closer to Bangor made things much easier – before that they lived in Flint Mountain. By then I'd developed a strong relationship with Andy and Steve, and was happy to be able to spend more time with them.

Although I was an adult, I still valued my close relationship with Nain and Taid Junction; both were really important to me and a strong influence. When I was on the nursing course I used to go there to do the garden and so on for them – but Taid preferred me to sit down with him, for hours sometimes, for a chat. I had tremendous respect for Taid and thought the world of him. He was a police sergeant in Conwy, and was known as 'Sarge' or 'Square' (because his name was Owen Owens, someone once told him in a maths lesson that he should be

Enjoying myself!

'Owen Squared' – and it stuck). After retiring from the police he took a warden's job in a big caravan park in Conwy where he had his own caravan, which is where we went every Easter and summer holiday. Nain and Taid's health deteriorated when they were in their eighties, and they both died within a day of each other. They were given a joint funeral, which was a very difficult experience, another loss.

There wasn't much stability at home in the Morgan Lloyd, but working behind the bar was tremendous fun as I'd have amusing conversations with some of the regulars, who included some very interesting characters. Working nights during the weekends was a different story as it got so busy – there'd be fighting and so on, and very drunk people making fools of themselves – but on the other hand a lot of pretty girls used to come into the bar! Sometimes there'd be a bit of a competition between myself and the other barmen to get girls to agree to a date ... and although I say it myself, I was quite successful at that!

Me, Gavin and James

Despite the fun and games, I realised that living in a pub wasn't something I could do long-term, so when I embarked on my nursing career I moved to live in the nurses' home, while still enjoying the occasional visit to the Morgan Lloyd.

I'd matured a great deal by the time I got to the end of my nurse training. By then I was 23 years old and had met Lisa, as I mentioned in the last chapter. She was a trainee teacher at Bangor University. Within the first year of our relationship Lisa was pregnant – which was quite a shock for her family, and for me – but by the end of her pregnancy everyone was thrilled to bits. 2 December 1994 was one of the best days of my life: Lois Angharad, my first child, was born, and I was over the moon. Adapting to fatherhood proved a very easy task and Lois brought enormous happiness to us and the rest of the family. We'd bought our first house in Lanfairpwll, Anglesey, and by the time Owen Rhys was born three years later – another very happy day in my life – we'd moved to a bigger house down the road. I was really happy – I had a daughter and son, both very different from each other, and unique characters. Three years later another baby, Beca Fflur, arrived, and the little family was complete.

Llanfairpwll was a lovely place to live, and had plenty going on there. I was chairman of the Nursery school committee and later chaired the PTA at Ysgol Llanfairpwll. By his fifth birthday Owen had taken up football, and as no-one else was willing to do it I started coaching his team, the Llanfair Hotshots, despite confessing to everyone that I no longer knew much about football. Luckily, Brian, one of the other parents, volunteered to help me, and the Hotshots enjoyed great success. During this period life was busy, between work pressures, Lisa's and my interests and the children's activities.

On the first of July 2003, the world stood still for a few seconds. I'd got home from work to a quiet house, with no sign of the usual welcome from the children. Lisa was waiting for

With Lois as a baby

me at the door. She told me straight away that Arwyn had died. I remember sitting at the foot of the stairs not knowing what else to do. Lisa had received a phone call from Steven, Arwyn's best friend, who'd found him in his bed and called for an ambulance which took Arwyn to Ysbyty Gwynedd. Mam and Clive were on holiday in France at the time, and Lisa'd had to phone them to break the news to them. I rushed to the casualty unit in Ysbyty Gwynedd and a nurse took me to see Arwyn. He looked very peaceful, and I kissed him on the head and said goodbye.

Arwyn's passing left a big gap in my life. We'd been very close as children, and the fact that we'd lived apart hadn't changed that. He'd had very difficult periods in his life, and suffered terribly with his health as he'd had difficulty managing his diabetes. When he was 21 he was diagnosed with epilepsy, although as a family we're sure that he'd had that affliction since childhood too. Arwyn often used to discuss his problems with me, and he admitted that he sometimes felt low – his inability to get a job contributed to this. But in the last year of his life things had started to look up for him. Off his own bat, he'd gone to the jobcentre in Bangor and started volunteering as a porter at Ysbyty Gwynedd. This opened a door for him and he was thrilled when he managed to get employed as a porter at the hospital. His confidence had returned and he was enjoying life again. Arwyn had two children, Luke and Holly, and although he wasn't in a relationship with their mother,

Melanie, they were on good terms and he loved them very much. Arwyn would be very proud today to see his children grown up to be polite and friendly young people.

One of the hardest things I've ever had to do was to tell Luke that his dad was dead. He cried out loud for a long time, holding on to me tightly. I'd also had to tell Dad that Arwyn had died, and it was an enormous shock for him too. That week was a busy one: organising the funeral and clearing Arwyn's house, as well as receiving many visitors who came to share their condolences with us. The funeral was massive, and seeing so many friends and family there was a great comfort. It took some time for things to settle down after Arwyn died – things were never going to be the same. I started looking at life differently, and became determined to make the most of every opportunity.

Without going into too much detail, as time went by I didn't feel happy in my marriage. I felt that Lisa and I were living separate lives to some extent, and in 2007 we separated. I went to live with Mam and Clive, who were living in Talwrn by then, and tried to get through a very difficult time. I was worried about how all this would affect the children, and I felt very guilty, although I saw the three of them very often and carried on with the school and village activities. There were times when the children were obviously sad, and that hurt, but all I could do was to emphasise that I loved them and would always be there for them. Unfortunately, Lisa and I weren't communicating very well in those early years, which didn't help the situation.

I'd met Becky through work and had fallen in love with her. She totally understood my situation, and realised that I needed to work on my relationship with the children. After living for eighteen months in Talwrn I moved in with Becky and soon the three had met her. It wasn't easy for her or the children, and it was a tough situation for me too. I felt as if I was in the middle trying to please everybody. Siôn Arwyn's arrival in 2009 was a big help in bringing everyone closer together – the three were delighted when he was born, and again twenty months later in 2011 when Ianto Huw came into the world.

Despite having had plenty of tough experiences during my life, I don't look back and feel that I had a bad deal. I firmly believe that I've enjoyed a very happy life – and the negative experiences have even influenced me and made me a stronger person. There are people in far worse situations than myself all over the world, and I try to remember that when I'm tempted to complain. My glass is always half-full, and I'm thankful that that's how I look at things.

Arwyn and I in 1996, at Clive's 50th birthday party

'I think I'm going to need your help pretty soon, Mans.' That's the first I heard of Irfon's health issues, back in December 2014. He had strong suspicions that he was suffering from bowel cancer and even though I tried to suggest that many other conditions could cause similar symptoms, Irfon, bless him, was pretty sure what the test results would show.

I've spent hours with Irfon and Becky over the last three years – trying to offer support and give practical help where needed. Looking back over that period of appointments and different procedures, my mind always returns to that horribly difficult day and night in Aintree Hospital, Liverpool, when Irfon was in the hands of his consultant Mr Malik, having major liver surgery.

Irfon and Becky had travelled up to Liverpool early that morning, and Sarah, one of Becky's closest friends, and myself were intending to join Becky in order to keep her company whilst Irfon was in theatre. When Sarah and I arrived, Becky and Irfon had just said their goodbyes and she was in tears; we decided to drive to a nearby shopping centre – Becky and I knew we had a long, harrowing day ahead of us.

After a spot of lunch in Frankie and Benny's, lots of talk about nothing in particular and a visit to Marks & Spencer's, we returned to Aintree. It was around four in the afternoon, and we decided to go and get the keys to the room Becky had arranged to stay in that night. After that was sorted, down we went to the café for a cuppa – and I'm sure one became five!

By ten that night there was still no news about Irfon and the strain was starting to take its toll on Becky so we decided to walk towards the intensive care department in case they had any news. 'They must be getting ready to bring Irfon back as they've asked us to take his bed down. You're welcome to sit in the family room and we'll come for you when there's more news,' they told us. We were faced with more waiting and even more coffee!

Around midnight, the call came from Mr Malik, and Becky could hardly hold the phone as she was shaking like a leaf. The surgery had gone as well as Mr Malik had expected it to, but Irfon was experiencing the side-effects of a long and difficult operation. Half an hour later, Mr Malik came down to talk to us in order to explain what he had done, and he had a very serious look on his face when he told us, 'we have to get Irfon through the night, his body is suffering the effects of the surgery and we will have to keep him on a ventilator for the next few hours.'

True to form, Becky found strength from somewhere, and we set off to Intensive Care to see Irfon – seeing him there was hard, and when Becky held his hand and told him she loved him very much and that Mr Malik had successfully completed the operation, Irfon started stirring to the point that the nurses had to increase his sedation. I'd never seen such a thing happen before!

Irfon is an unique and very special person, and when he asked me to write this piece, he told me, 'I don't want some garbage about inspiration and stuff, OK?' How could anyone write about him without using that word? He's also kind, wise, loving, mischievous and extremely brave. It's an honour and a pleasure being your friend, Irfs. Thank you.

Manon Williams, Friend and Betsi Cadwaladr University Health Board Cancer Care Matron

Chapter 4

On the Other Side

Right, let's go back to 2014, and after a busy time with the wedding and the rugby trip to Dublin straight afterwards I was keen to start the treatment. I had a meeting with the doctor on Alaw ward on Tuesday morning, 11 February, and he explained everything to me. I faced three months of chemotherapy, and although apprehensive I felt positive and confident that the treatment would be successful. Furthermore, I was determined to remain strong throughout. Becky felt the same – full of energy and ready for it. After the meeting I went back to the waiting room and waited to be called in to start the chemo.

I'll never forget that waiting room – I'm sure I spent hours there during those first few months. There was a huge fish tank, posters and forms all over the walls, and the Alaw Day Unit reception area facing it. The reception staff always had time for a chat, and many a time I saw one or two of them comfort a patient who was either poorly or had just received bad news. One of them was called Roxy, and I remember her sitting with me one afternoon when I was upset about something. Nothing was too much trouble for them, which made things much easier if you needed to call in to enquire about something, as I often had to during my treatment.

In the waiting room I met other patients, and many of us would discuss our situation, share the side-effects of the chemo, compare our eating habits (or inability to eat) and how we were coping generally. The main topic of conversation for the female patients was their wigs, as hair loss is a side-effect of cancer treatments. It wasn't always obvious that someone was wearing a wig as they looked so natural. I admired these women's bravery – it's hard enough to deal with having cancer, not to mention hair loss, and I'm sure that the psychological effect of that can be considerable. I asked whether I was likely to lose my hair but the chemo I was about to receive didn't cause that. Chemotherapy has developed amazingly over the years and now there are different kinds that target specific cancers. Of course, there are still side-effects, and I was about to discover how bad they could be.

The cancer doctors' clinic was located in the same place, and sitting in the waiting room before seeing the doctor could be a horrible time. The worst part was waiting for the results of a scan or blood test, and as I experienced before the diagnosis, time seemed to slow down when I was waiting for news. Despite feeling positive about starting the treatment, naturally I was nervous too and a little apprehensive when trying to imagine what lay ahead of me. Becky was always good at setting my mind at rest, but of course she felt the same anxieties as I did.

I was called in by one of the nurses to quite a big room where the treatment was to take place, full of comfy chairs and about five beds, but according to one of the nurses it wasn't big enough. She explained to me that there had been plenty of room in the unit years ago, but as so many more people are receiving treatment these days space was at a premium, and plans were afoot to build a new, bigger unit. I soon saw how busy it was – with patients coming and going all day and nurses working methodically and efficiently. First of all, Becky and I had a cup of tea and a biscuit. There was a drinks machine in the unit and everyone was welcome to help themselves. The drinks and biscuits were funded by charitable donations, and everyone was very glad of them. I was given a bowl of warm water to immerse my hands in so that my veins would stand out, as I needed to have blood extracted and have a needle inserted in my hand to receive the medication. After all this was done, Chas, the Chemotherapy Specialist Nurse, came to me to explain that I'd spend four hours receiving the medication on the unit and be given a fortnight's course of tablets to take home with me. Then I'd have a week with no treatment at all, before going back to start the cycle all over again. As for side-effects, he explained that I'd feel tired and would suffer from peripheral neuropathy, which is a feeling of pins and needles, mainly in my hands and feet. It was important to keep an eye on the blood levels too, she said, as there was a risk of infection.

When the drug started entering my system I experienced a burning sensation, and an uncomfortable feeling as it made its way up my arm. The nurses kept a close watch on me and assessed me frequently by measuring my blood pressure and so on. I was given a special plastic mat to warm my arm and ease the discomfort, which was a great help.

To be honest I wasn't sure what kind of atmosphere to expect on the unit. I've discussed this with a few people in recent years, people who feared that everyone would be quite downhearted there. There *are* sad times, of course, and getting to know someone on the unit and then hearing of their death never gets any easier. This has happened to me once or twice, and that kind of thing makes me worry about my own situation. Although I tried to keep positive, experiences like this shook me, and I had to work hard to focus on being positive again. But the truth is that the atmosphere on the unit isn't all doom and gloom. The nurses appear happy at work, the patients chat amongst each other and it can be quite jolly there at times. I remember once sitting next to a lady in her eighties while we were receiving our treatments. She was in very high spirits and was a bit of a character, looking forward to completing her chemo course as she was going abroad on holiday. I started pulling her leg, asking her if she'd got her bikini ready, and there was great hilarity in the unit when she revealed, 'I don't need a bikini, I'll be skinny dipping'! There's a certain camaradarie amongst cancer patients that's hard to describe, but I always felt it strongly on Alaw.

It was difficult to get used to the experience of being a nurse and a patient. I thought I'd have been a bit more inquisitive than I was, but I have to say that the unit staff's nursing skills were exceptionally good. As I'd been working in the community for so many years the nurses didn't know me, but they soon started to be amazed at how many visitors I had while receiving my treatment, including quite a large number of hospital staff members. Gary was a frequent visitor, of course, and I'm sure all the nurses knew him as he'd worked in the hospital for such a long time. During her lunch hour Karen, a nurse who'd been a friend of mine for years, used to visit, Nerys Haf regularly popped by for a chat as her office was on the unit, and Manon Ogwen also dropped in occasionally to keep an eye on me. Sharon Thomas used to call often as well to see how Becky and I were. Sharon was a senior manager in the health board and has been a really good friend to us as a family.

After years of working in the mental health field I was very keen to erase the stigma attached to the subject. One source of disappointment to me throughout my career was the nurse training structure – mental health nurses were responsible for mental health problems and mental illness, while general nurses (or adult nurses as they're known today) looked after physical illnesses or conditions. In reality, of course, it's impossible to separate the two, and I believe that nurse training should look closely at this situation. Becky very soon noticed that no doctor or nurse had asked specifically about my mental health – but although they didn't realise it, every one of the nurses on Alaw ward was doing mental health work naturally by showing emotional care and so on. Research shows that a high percentage of cancer patients suffer from mental health problems, especially severe anxiety and depression, and that men are less willing to admit to this than women.

My own mental health was in good condition at this time, and I'd started practising mindfulness again. This is a technique that developed originally from Buddhism, which has now developed to be part of the daily practice of a great number of people throughout the UK, and Bangor University is at the cutting edge. About a year after Arwyn died Mam and I attended a mindfulness course for twelve weeks, and we both benefitted greatly from it. It took time for me to get used to the practices, and Mam was hugely embarrassed once or twice as I fell asleep during the sessions and started snoring like a pig all over the room while everyone else was trying their best to relax!

I'd known John Hughes since our days as student nurses, and now he was working as a Complementary Therapist, offering his service to cancer patients on Alaw. Initially I had weekly appointments with John to work on relaxation techniques. John used scripts which helped me think pleasant

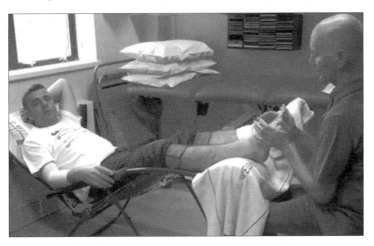

Complementary therapy at the hands of John

thoughts, slow down my breathing and relax the muscles. He also prepared CDs for me to listen to at home, and sometimes Becky and I would lie down in our conservatory listening to one of them and enjoying relaxing together. Doing this as well as practising mindfulness was a great help to keep us feeling positive and dealing with the strain of my illness. Getting to sleep at night was easy now, and despite the side-effects I felt I was coping well.

When someone is diagnosed with cancer a lot of people offer advice on what's best to do. It's natural for everyone to want to look for answers, but listening to every piece of advice and accepting all suggestions, from friends and on the internet, is a very dangerous thing. Becky and I went through a spell of trawling the internet for different treatments and reading about other people's experiences. Unfortunately, it was very hard to remain positive when I read some of the stories as some of them were awfully negative.

Lots of people contacted me to urge me to try different things. I didn't disregard anybody, but I decided not to try most of them. Many said that cannabis can treat cancer, and as I understand it there is some evidence to support this. Another suggestion was apricot kernels, and one kind gentleman sent some for me to try (but I didn't). Someone else suggested that a daily spoonful of kerosene (which is engine oil) had worked in some countries ... I decided not to try that either! Of course, I was very grateful to everyone for thinking about me.

One suggestion I did try was drinking vegetable juice. Some argued strongly that drinking it every day had got rid of cancer, and others believed that it at least reduced tumours and kept cancer under control. There was nothing to lose by giving it a go. Although I didn't believe that the juice would cure the cancer it was healthy, and it might help with the blood's iron levels and keep infections away. Becky bought a very expensive juicer, and immediately set about preparing a drink for me every day. Well, I have to admit, it may have been healthy but it didn't taste good. I'm sure I was like a naughty little boy waiting for his spoonful of nasty medicine from Nain in the old days, as I sat in the kitchen staring at the glass before plucking up the courage to drink it! Kale, beetroot, cucumber and celery juice is not something I'd recommend to anybody on account of its flavour, but having said that, I still drink kale juice daily to this day and it hasn't done me any harm!

After every cycle of chemotherapy the neuropathy, or feeling of pins and needles, affected me more and more. Walking out to the car after the first treatment I felt as if my throat was starting to freeze due to the cold air – a really unpleasant experience. From then on, after spending a day on Alaw, I had to wear a scarf over my mouth to go out into the fresh air. Drinking cold drinks was impossible too, which I sometimes forgot. My hands and feet suffered too, and I had to wear gloves constantly. I couldn't go to the fridge to get milk to make a cup of tea (which was a good excuse!). Unfortunately, there was a possibility that the neuropathy would affect me forever, but the symptoms have diminished substantially by now, thank goodness, except on very cold days when my feet still hurt.

The name of the drug I received in the hospital was Oxaliplatin, and the tablets I took at home were called Capecitabine. During the first week of treatment I was always very tired, and spent a lot of time sleeping on the sofa during the day. Thanks mainly to Becky, I got up every morning, had a shower, got dressed and went downstairs to have breakfast and take my tablets. It would have been so easy to just stay in bed, but that wouldn't have done me any good. I'd have the chemo on Mondays, and I wouldn't recover properly until the weekend. By the second week I was able to do more; I'd go out for a walk and some fresh air regularly. By the third week I was more or less fine, and made the most of that week before starting the cycle again on the following Monday. I had three months of that treatment, and I think we coped well as a family.

There were various people on hand to offer help in their own way, for which we were really grateful. Becky's friends, Nia and Gwawr, used to come over to see us often, bringing cakes or a saucepan of soup. Gwenllïan (or Llian as she is known), a colleague of mine at CAMHS, was a regular visitor too. Her soup was very nice but her pear crumble was delicious! Friends of the family were very supportive – not only to us but to Mam and Clive too. I could list names all day here, but I won't as you all know very well who you are.

I remember sitting on the sofa during the first week of a chemo cycle and finding it hard to stay awake. I didn't say much at times like these, which was very hard for Becky. I often wonder what effect this had on Siôn and Ianto, and I remember feeling guilty. Nevertheless, by the second and third weeks I was able to pay attention to them and live a fairly normal life. The situation was the same with the older children too – by the second weekend they could come and stay over for the weekend without any problem.

Talking to them was still difficult. Beca was the one who came to stay most and she was quite happy; she didn't ask many questions but was happy to listen as I explained various things to her. I was seeing Owen less frequently as he started socialising more and more with his friends, but he never asked about my illness or the treatment – that was his way of dealing with things. Lois asked a lot of questions and felt happier when she was told everything.

I placed great emphasis on keeping positive and mentally healthy. When I was well enough, the weekend would be sure to include a trip out with the family, and on Sunday mornings I'd go down to Bangor Rugby Club to coach the youngsters. About a year previously I'd started rugby sessions for

The boys, Siôn and Ianto, and I in our rugby shirts

youngsters aged three to six. The idea was to attract young families down to the club, and give them a bit of fun ... and personally I was trying not to let Siôn and Ianto develop too much of an interest in football! When Owen was young he showed an interest in all sports and played rugby and football. Although I couldn't give one hundred percent to the rugby sessions I loved being there, except when it was windy and cold. The neuropathy kicked in then, and my face would feel all prickly while my nose felt as if it was frozen solid! As I couldn't go to the club every week, one of the mothers, Claire, took responsibility for the sessions and she's still there today doing a great job.

Keeping in touch with friends was important to me, and regular visits by some of the lads gave me great pleasure, but unfortunately, at times, Becky had to turn people away because I was so exhausted. Some of their responses surprised me – one of the old rugby lads, Paul McLennan, explained that he'd been scared of coming to see me for the first time because he didn't know exactly what to expect. Many people imagine that all cancer sufferers lose their hair, are thin and look ill, but neither my appearance nor my behaviour had changed, which was a great relief for first-time visitors like Paul. People's reactions out on the street or in shops were interesting too, and people I didn't know that well would find it very difficult to know how to respond. I remember being out shopping one day with Becky, and I was pushing the trolley. A woman approached me – I knew her, but not very well – and put her hand on my shoulder, leaned her head to one side, pursed her lips and looked at me with a sad look without saying a word, before walking away! I didn't know what to say or do except laugh!

By April 2014 the first round of treatment had ended, and I had numerous scans to assess how effective the chemo had been. Once again, it was time for us to wait for the results. I tried my best not to dwell on them, but it was hard not to worry. Thankfully, the doctor had good news for me – the chemo had been successful and the two tumours in the liver had shrunk.

The next part of the treatment was radiotherapy, at Ysbyty Glan Clwyd in Bodelwyddan. Unfortunately, there was a waiting list for that and I'd have to be patient. I was a bit apprehensive, and worried that the tumours in the liver would grow back in the meantime. The doctor explained that it would take at least eight weeks before that would happen, and that she hoped that I could start on the treatment within that time.

I'd said when Arwyn died that I'd like to organise a charitable activity in his memory to mark the tenth anniversary of his passing and celebrate his life. It was 11 years since his death, and I'd decided that the time was right. The family weren't keen for me to do this, especially on my own, in view of everything that was going on, but I grasped the opportunity between the two treatments to arrange a charity evening to be held in April 2014. As I was so adamant, Mam and Clive agreed to help with the arrangements. A year previously I'd discussed my wish with my friend Robin McBryde, who agreed to be guest speaker at an evening in Bangor Rugby Club. I'd also contacted Rupert Moon, who was working in the North at the time as Director of North Wales Rugby. Robin and Rupert were good friends since their playing days with Llanelli years ago, and the idea of a kind of double act appealed to me. After a discussion with Mam we decided that all the profit would be given to the epilepsy charity SUDEP (Sudden Unexplained Death due to Epilepsy).

After the hours spent organising the evening, it arrived very quickly. On the preceding afternoon, Mam and I were interviewed by the popular Welsh language singer and TV presenter Elin Fflur about Arwyn's life and death, the purpose of the evening and so on. The interview was broadcast on the *Prynhawn Da* programme on S4C the next day while Mam, Clive and some of their friends were running around making the last-minute arrangements. Becky's stepfather Dylan's company had agreed to sponsor the evening, and we were also supported by local companies like Paddy's pub in Bangor and Morgan Evans (who conducted the auction) and the rugby club who gave us use of the clubhouse free of charge. The items on auction were worth bidding for and the tickets were sold out.

It proved to be an excellent, entertaining evening, and I suspect that I was the only one sober by the end of the night! Robin gave a brilliant talk and spoke from the heart, and Rupert was very comical heckling Robin – the double act was a success. It was an incredible feeling to discover that over five thousand pounds had been collected on the night.

Around about the same time a young man called Stephen Sutton was getting a lot of attention in the national press. He was raising thousands of pounds for a young people's cancer charity by completing a load of activities such as parachuting and bungee jumping. He himself suffered from bowel cancer and was an inspiration to many with his positive attitude despite being aware that he was dying, as no treatment had succeeded in getting rid of the cancer. Stephen died that May, and once again he received plenty of attention – not only because of the money he'd raised but also for raising awareness of cancer amongst young people. On the night Stephen died I received a phone call from Radio Cymru asking whether I'd be willing to speak on Dylan Jones' morning programme about my experience of living with bowel cancer and my feelings about Stephen Sutton's death. Of course, I agreed to be on the programme as I felt strongly that it was necessary to raise awareness and share positivity, and if Stephen Sutton had managed to do that up to his final days the least I could do was to follow in his footsteps.

I'd spoken on radio and television many times before by virtue of my post as CAMHS manager, but had never spoken

With broadcaster Dylan Jones after my radio interview

publicly before about such a personal matter. I was welcomed at the BBC studio in Bangor and saw many familiar faces there, which made me feel at home. Dylan Jones was great and the interview went very well although it lasted far longer than I'd anticipated. During the interview I spoke honestly about the diagnosis and my feelings, the charity evening in memory of Arwyn and, of course, my recent wedding (although I almost forgot to mention that despite Dylan's prompting!). I talked about the inspiration Stephen

Sutton had given me and the fantastic feeling I'd had whilst raising money, and without a second thought I announced, live on the radio, that I was going to shave my head and wear a different funny wig every day for a whole fortnight in order to raise awareness and raise funds for cancer patients in the Alaw Unit. When I got home Becky was in slight shock, but there was no changing my mind after such a public announcement, made without first discussing it with her!

After I shaved my head in aid of #teamirfon

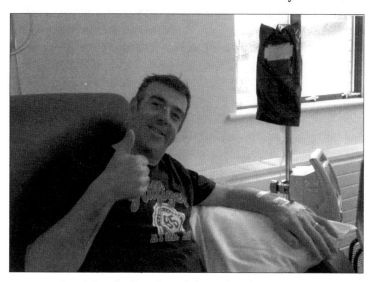

Receiving the first dose of chemo in February 2014

We were married by then, of course, but we'd never got formally engaged, as we'd got married in a hurry. I'd decided to buy Becky an engagement ring, and had saved money to do so. In early May 2014, the four of us went with Dylan and Glenna (Becky's mother and stepfather), to Spain for a week between chemotherapy sessions. While we were there, Becky and I went off to buy the engagement ring. That evening, I'd booked a table for the two of us in one of our favourite restaurants on the square in the lovely village of Benalmadena. While we were sitting at the table, I told Becky to give me her wedding ring, and I put it, with my own wedding ring, in my pocket. After finishing the meal, I went down on one knee with the engagement ring and said to her, 'I love you. Thank you so much for being my wife.' By then we were giggling like little children, and I kissed her. The rest of the customers started celebrating with us once they realised what was going on – and made sure that she'd accepted the proposal! The restaurant owner brought us a big bottle of Champagne, and two glasses. As I wasn't allowed to drink Becky asked for glasses for everyone. I felt guilty about all this attention because we were deceiving them, in a way!

*At Llanddwyn beach –
the best place in the world*

⊱⊰

I first met Irfon over 20 years ago, when he was a paediatric nurse looking after my daughter. Even then he was a bit unusual, everything you would expect from a children's nurse but with an extra dose of charisma and the ability to relate to a child in exactly the right way; in this case with humour.

Our paths crossed professionally many times over the years, as he moved into child and adolescent mental health services, eventually becoming a much respected manager. He had the ability to make all his colleagues feel listened to and come up with solutions that were fair. It hardly needs saying how many young people and families he helped during his career; I often meet parents who still say how he gave them hope when all seemed hopeless and young people, who are now parents themselves, speak of him with warmth and affection, and of how he turned things round for them.

When Irfon was diagnosed with cancer, the shock waves rippled through all the communities he was part of and the outpouring of love was astonishing . In typical style, he got on with the job and, despite his illness, set about raising funds for others in the same situation, making life a little more bearable. Again, the success of #team irfon is a testament to the man himself, people just simply wanted to do something, anything, to help and make a difference.

As Irfon's illness progressed, he was forced to move to England to have a drug that was not available to him in Wales. This became the impetus for the Hawl i fyw /Fighting Chance campaign. The campaign aimed to gain cross party support to end the post code lottery and end the unfair 'exceptionality' clause that prevented people getting life saving drugs. The success of the campaign has been well documented but I am sure people would be surprised to know that there was no slick PR machine behind it, just people who wanted to see change and who were prepared to work for it, not just for Irfon but everybody in Wales. Irfon would be the first to acknowledge the 'behind the scenes' work that it took to make the campaign such a success, but without his and Becky's willingness to share their story, it would not have happened. At times the media attention was overwhelming for them and we questioned whether we should go on, but whatever personal crises were happening (and there were many) they were determined that despite the cost to themselves, it must continue.

Irfon has received many accolades and awards; all of them well deserved. I think the highest accolade anyone can achieve is to live their life according to their beliefs and principles, not wavering in the face of adversity. He has shown us all his courage, his dignity and determination. He has been passionate about the things he believed in, in every area of his life. For those of us lucky enough to call him our friend, he has shown us kindness and fun, lots of fun. Even in the darkest days, there has been laughter. I have seen him love and be loved, achieve incredible things and most importantly I have witnessed him be the change he wanted to see in the world. Not bad for a cheeky Welsh lad and an average Scrabble player!

I am reminded of the quote , 'People will forget what you said, people will forget what you did, but people will never forget how you made them feel.'

You make us feel special, important, listened to, loved. I hope you feel all those things from us, your friends.

Dr Liz Whitehead

Chapter 5

Awyr Las (Blue Sky)

After the big announcement about shaving my head, I arranged to meet Kirsty Thompson, manager of Awyr Las, the North Wales NHS charity. The charity's purpose is to raise money to pay for things over and above what the NHS can fund. Wigs are one example of this in the Alaw unit, and having seen the difference wigs made for patients, I was keen to help the cause and raise money for these, and loads of other things. Becky and I had discussed setting a target of five thousand pounds, but at the meeting Kirsty suggested that we could raise a lot more than that, so we decided on a target of twenty thousand pounds. That sum sounded enormous, and we both started to feel quite nervous, thinking we'd take a long time to raise so much money. We discussed the idea of shaving off my hair and Kirsty suggested doing it at the Urdd Eisteddfod (the annual Welsh language youth festival) that year, outside the Awyr Las tent. She said that she'd ask the singer Rhys Meirion and Rhun ap Iorwerth, the Welsh Assembly Member for Anglesey, to be part of the event as they were ambassadors of the charity. Kirsty named the campaign #teamirfon (#tîmirfon in Welsh). I didn't think twice at the time about being the name and face for such a campaign, because I never imagined that it would develop to be so big and get so much hype.

The Urdd Eisteddfod was held in Bala that year, and on the Tuesday, 27 May 2014, we went there for the day. Mam and Clive and Dylan and Glenna came to support us too, and when the time came for me have my head shaved quite a crowd of people were assembled outside the tent. I knew a lot of them – the event had been publicised on Facebook and on Radio

Cymru. Rhun ap Iorwerth was at the mic, talking about Awyr Las, urging people to come and watch and asking them to contribute towards the good cause. We had a quick interview to allow me to explain my story and my desire to support the charity before Rhys Meirion got to work with the shaver. Mam's face was a picture as the hair fell away and Becky was laughing, and itching to have a go with the shaving machine. Rhys joked that he'd never shaved anyone's head before but that he'd sheared sheep in the past, which was quite a similar experience! In no time at all, the hair was all gone and my head felt quite cold. The first wig I wore was a very funny one: a massive brown curly afro-style wig, and I spent the rest of the day walking around the field with it on my head. Siôn and Ianto were very amused and Becky was still unable to believe that she was going to spend an entire fortnight with me in a different wig every day. A lot of people gave me astonished looks – some laughed at me, others looked gobsmacked, and one man even asked me if it was my own hair!

I wore all kinds of wigs over that fortnight, from multi-coloured curly wigs to pink girly ones and a red and black Mohican. People's reactions were very varied. Some would come up to me laughing and donate money to the cause while others asked what I was doing, but I used to laugh when people looked at me, said nothing and carried on as if nothing was amiss! Every day for those two weeks a photo of me was put on the Awyr Las Facebook page, with messages about helping cancer patients. I had loads of fun with the wigs and it was obvious that the stunt had helped enormously to raise awareness of the campaign as well as the charity.

Dad decided to do the 'wigathon' after my fortnight was up, to show his support for me. An event was held outside the Morgan Lloyd pub where he had his head shaved, and Siôn and Ianto were well chuffed when they got a go with the shaver to shave Taid's head. Dad wearing his wigs was a hilarious sight.

Dad and I in our wigs

Over 4,000 people in North Wales are diagnosed with cancer every year

Mae dros 4,000 o bobl yng Ngogledd Cymru yn cael diagnosis o ganser bob blwyddyn

#teamirfon

Thank you so much for your support.

Diolch am eich cefnogaeth.

#teamirfon

Dad's a taxi driver in Caernarfon and I received a few reports from people who had seen him drive by wearing the weirdest wigs. I don't know if business went down during that fortnight – certainly, I wouldn't have got into a taxi driven by a man wearing a big curly bright yellow wig! Between us, we managed to raise nearly five thousand pounds during the first month of #teamirfon and it became evident that the cause, namely supporting the needs of local cancer sufferers, was one that was very close to the community's heart.

Suddenly, loads of people started getting in touch with offers to support the cause. Llanfairpwll Juniors Football Club arranged a charity match, and John Pierce Jones and Llion Williams (aka the popular characters Arthur Picton and George from S4C's football comedy *C'mon Midffild*) came to support the event. Llion and I have been friends since we both took part in a TV programme about mental health a few years back, and he's kept in touch with me throughout my illness. Elin Fflur had arranged for a film crew from the magazine programme *Heno* on S4C to be there too, and the event attracted quite a bit of attention, succeeding in raising over two thousand pounds. Various people were fundraising by running races, and one of my neighbours, Carl Thatcher, set himself a challenge to run a number of races. The challenges people set themselves were becoming increasingly difficult and unbelievable. My friend Alan Owen completed the Iron Man

Alan Owen after one of his challenges

in Tenby one week. After that he climbed the Five Peaks with Stephen Edwards, Gwyn Griffiths and Irfon Davies, supported by Big Kev who drove them from location to location in a van. The lads started at Pen y Fan, then went up Cader Idris, Snowdon, Scafell Pike in the north of England before finishing on Ben Nevis in Scotland, all in 36 hours! Following this, there were races every week for a month, ending with the Bangor 10K race, which Becky ran too.

All these charity events gave us a positive focus, and I enjoyed it tremendously. Of course, my treatment was still ongoing, and during June and July I received radiotherapy on a daily basis (excluding weekends) for five weeks. I had to travel to Ysbyty Glan Clwyd in Bodelwyddan every day to receive that treatment, about 34 miles away from Bangor. I didn't find the journey too strenuous to be honest, but I felt sorry for those who had to come from distant places like Pen Llŷn and Meirionnydd. Before starting on that radiotherapy, I met the consultant who was responsible for that part of the treatment. He explained everything in detail, saying that I'd be assessed by the radiographer and have two small 'tattoos' on my stomach to enable them to target the location of the tumour precisely. He also explained that there would be side-effects – to tell you the truth I didn't hear what half of them were as I had such a fright when he mentioned the possibility that I'd be impotent after the treatment, as they were targeting a spot that was close to the nerves of my reproductive system. I left the room sweating buckets, and Becky said that my reaction was worse than when I was told that I had cancer in the first place! The radiotherapy service was very slick, and I was lucky to get an appointment slot first thing in the morning, at 9.15 every day. I had to get up early to have breakfast and get myself ready to leave the house before 8.30. Sometimes my friend Manon Ogwen would be going to Glan Clwyd to attend meetings, and

The Radiotherapy Department nurses

on those occasions I travelled with her, and had a cup of tea after the treatment while I waited for her to finish her meeting before setting off back to Bangor.

Halfway through the treatment I had an appointment with the consultant to see how I was getting on. Becky was with me, and while we were waiting, I popped to the loo. While I was there, a man sitting next to Becky asked her, 'What's the matter with your father?' She found it quite amusing, and she's often reminded me of the incident. I knew I looked ill, but I didn't think I was that bad!

After getting accustomed to the treatment and seeing that I wasn't suffering any side-effects (including that important one, I'm glad to say!) I started driving myself there daily. I very rarely had to wait more than fifteen minutes for the treatment. The staff were brilliant; they were professional and straightforward and were very nice people too. The treatment itself only took about five minutes, and then I was free to return home. As everyone's appointments were at the same time every day, I got to know the other patients who were there at the same time as me. One lady in her eighties was there with her sister, and the two of them loved teasing me that they wanted me as a toy boy. The five weeks soon passed, and it was time for me to have another scan to see if the chemo and radiotherapy had worked.

Once again it was time to wait in the waiting room in Ysbyty Gwynedd's Alaw unit for the scan results. Dr Bale called us in to his room. Good news! The treatment had succeeded in reducing the tumour in the bowel and the two in the liver. This was excellent news, of course, and meant that I'd be able to have an operation on the liver first, in Liverpool, and another on the bowel a short while afterwards in Bangor.

During this period Mr Bhalerao, the consultant I'd seen initially, had referred me to a specialist in Liverpool. Aintree Hospital is the specialist centre for liver treatments for north Wales and the surgeon there was called Mr Hassan Malik. As we researched his background on the internet it became evident that I was in safe hands – Mr Malik was prominent in his field and was world-renowned. I remember meeting him for the first time in Liverpool to discuss the operation I was about to have. It's funny how you create a mental picture of someone before meeting them – he was totally different to what I'd expected. To start with, he had a strong Scottish accent! He was a really nice man, and I felt perfectly at ease in his company. He took his time showing me a scan of my liver before explaining what he was going to do. He'd obviously realised that I was anxious to buy as much time as I could, and he was willing to push the boundaries to ensure that I succeeded. Immediately, he allayed any worries Becky and I might have had, and I developed a great respect for him. He introduced us to Specialist Nurse Claire Burston, and took us to another room to describe the process I'd have to go through prior to the operation. Of course, we didn't realise at the time what an important part these two would play in our lives for the next two years.

I felt very positive; the pain had almost disappeared thanks to the chemo and radiotherapy. I wasn't constipated (which made things much easier) and my mental health was in good condition. I was sleeping well, eating and enjoying socialising with family and friends. By now, a lot of people were following my progress on Facebook and loads of people added me as a 'friend' although many were strangers to me. I was receiving endless messages from people saying that I'd been a great help to them by being open about my cancer, and that my positive outlook had inspired them or their family members. These messages made me feel very happy, despite thinking that I wasn't doing anything really special. One thing that grew in popularity during that summer was my '100 Happy Days' on Facebook. I'd posted a picture that had made me happy that day every day for one hundred days. My intention was to focus on being positive and to urge everyone to realise how important it is to appreciate things in life, to make the most of every minute and to understand that good things happen every day,

One of my favourite '100 Happy Days' photos

and that it's just a matter of paying attention to them. My pictures varied from day to day: a selfie of myself and Becky at the seaside, a picture of the boys walking to school with a short message explaining what a privilege it was to be able to do that every day. Amongst the images were a picture of a beautiful flower, a photo of a blackberry tart before I ate it, a picture of me with Lois, Owen and Beca and a picture of the sunset over Puffin Island, off the coast of Anglesey.

I received a lot of messages that brought tears to my eyes. Many of my former patients got in touch to wish me well, saying what an influence I'd had on their lives. One man sent a picture of a story he'd written about me in school after a period in hospital, when he'd been a child in my care. More and more people were contacting me too with ideas for ways to raise money for the cause and by July the campaign had easily passed the target, with almost £30,000 raised. Hearing that gave me a massive shock – #teamirfon had now grown to be much bigger than Becky and I had ever imagined.

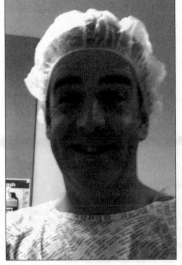

Before the first liver resection operation

I was given a date to go to Liverpool for the surgery to remove the tumours from the liver –1 August 2014 – but I had to go there for a day the week before that for a pre-op, which consisted of various tests to prepare for the operation. I was weighed and measured, had blood taken, a heart test and one completely unexpected test, namely a fitness test on a bike! This was fun, actually – wires were fitted onto me to measure my heartbeat and before starting I had to have a series of breathing tests, blowing into a pipe until I was completely out of breath. While on the bike I wore a tight plastic mask over my mouth. Riding the bike was easy to begin with, but as I pedalled it got increasingly difficult, and I was getting tired, fighting for breath and feeling my legs hurting. As if that wasn't enough, I had to do the breath test a few times again afterwards! I felt better when I realised that I was the youngest person in the room by a long stretch, and that some of the men could hardly walk, let alone ride a bike!

After all the tests I was interviewed by a nurse, who explained everything to me about the treatment procedure, and met the anaesthetist, Dr Carmen – a very nice Spanish lady who made me feel great. Reading the result of the bike test she asked me, 'Are you an athlete?' I was dead chuffed! Maybe she wasn't entirely serious, but I was grateful that I'd kept fairly fit all my life, and had carried on running and going to the gym even after giving up playing rugby.

31 July came very quickly. Mr Malik's secretary had arranged for us to stay at the Hospital Hotel that night as I'd need to be in the hospital by 7.30 the next morning. The word 'hotel' was a bit misleading – it was a room without a lock containing two beds (with hospital bedlinen on them). There was a bathroom with a shower, and it was quite adequate for us to get some sleep, rather than have to travel from Bangor in the early hours of the morning. I didn't sleep much that night – not because I was apprehensive, but in case I overslept ... the same feeling as I get before catching an early flight to go on holiday.

The next morning, I started to feel quite anxious, although I tried to hide it from Becky. She, I learnt later, felt the same, but didn't want to let on to me! After a quick shower I got dressed, and up we went to the theatre waiting area. Unfortunately, Becky wasn't allowed to stay there with me and I had to say goodbye to her before going in.

The nurses there were welcoming, but were obviously busy.

After a few quick tests, blood pressure and so on, I was taken to another office where one of Mr Malik's team was waiting for me. He was a New Zealander, and of course, we started talking about rugby. He said that his grandfather had played for the All Blacks, and when I Googled it a few days later, I found that he was telling the truth! Following a chat with him, Dr Carmen, the anaesthetist, explained how they would control the pain after the op. She told me that a bed had been reserved in the intensive care unit in case I needed it, and that made me a little more apprehensive. A friend of ours, Liz Whitehead, had asked me to send her a photo of myself in the paper nightie and hat I had to wear in the theatre, and one of the nurses looked at me in astonishment when I asked her to take a photo of me from behind with my backside in view. I sent Liz the image, as she'd promised me that she wouldn't share it with anyone, especially on Facebook! Moments later, I was lying on the operating table with doctors and nurses around me. I was given an injection in the back of my hand and an oxygen mask was placed on my face, and before I could count to five I was fast asleep.

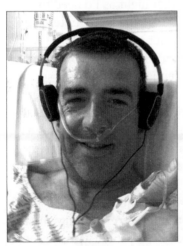

After my liver operation in Aintree, August 2014

Becky waited for four hours in the 'hotel' room for the call to tell her that the operation was over, and that I'd been moved to Ward 4. This was my first time on this ward, and I didn't realise at the time how well I would get to know the nurses there. I can't remember much more about that day, but I was informed that the operation had been successful, and that every bit of the cancer had been removed.

The next morning, I woke up

feeling so-so. I had a morphine pump to kill the pain, although I didn't use it much, a plaster down the middle of my belly and a catheter to pass water, which felt quite unpleasant. I had a hell of a shock when the nurse came to me. His name was Mark; he was a local man with a strong accent who was obviously a bit of a case but very friendly. He told me I had to get up out of bed, and to begin with I thought he was pulling my leg. But five minutes later, I was sitting in a chair with a bowl in front of me washing and shaving, with a little bit of help from Mark. Ward 4 practises what's known as enhanced care, and according to Mark, research shows that the sooner you start moving about after surgery the better. A physiotherapist came to see me that morning too, and walked me up and down the corridor. I was urged to do that at least four times a day in those early days.

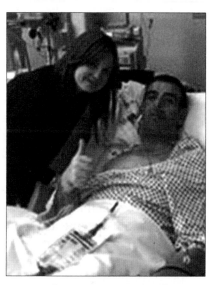

The operation went well

On Sunday, 3 August, a group of my friends were embarking on a challenge that was a bit bonkers, in my opinion. Dewi Morris, one of my friends from Llanfairpwll, came up with the idea of swimming across the Menai Straits to raise money for #teamirfon. The idea had ballooned within a few weeks, and a whole team of people were going to take the challenge including Paul McLennan, his son Sam, Anna Jones and Anna Morewood, my school friend Trystan Williams – and of course, Alan Owen. Trystan had invited a man named Alan Chambers to take part as well. Alan was ex-Army and had completed a lot of tough challenges, including walking to the North Pole. Kirsty from Awyr Las had invited actor Richard Harrington, best known for the drama *Hinterland*, to take part too. Neither Alan nor Richard had understood the dangers of the Straits, and although they completed the challenge, they both said that it was the hardest thing they'd ever done. Richard Harrington also apparently said that swimming the Menai Straits was much harder than running a marathon in the Sahara!!

When I got the story and pictures it was obvious that the weather was atrocious and that the Menai currents were particularly strong that day. Dewi Morris was first in, followed by everyone else, with the safety boats making sure that everyone was protected all the way. From what I heard, the Health and Safety people were doubtful whether the challenge should go ahead because of the stormy weather, but the gang jumped in and went for it anyway! The swim finished under Bangor pier, and it was nice to hear that the Pier was full of people who'd come to support the swimmers, evidently appreciating the difficulty of what they'd just achieved. There was a big party afterwards, arranged by Hayley Meek, who ran the Boatyard pub at the time, and Dafydd Hardy, the prominent local estate agent, which included an auction of items donated by local businesses and some works by the artist Pete Jones. Naturally, I would have loved to be there, but as I said to Becky at the time, it was much better for me to be where I was, with the tumours removed.

By Monday 4 August I felt much better. The catheter and plaster on my belly were gone, and I no longer needed the morphine pump. When the doctors came on their rounds, they suggested that I'd be going home the following morning. As it was Siôn Arwyn's fifth birthday, I managed to persuade them to let me go home that day instead. I called Becky to tell her the good news, and as Alan Owen was coming to see me that afternoon anyway, he agreed to drive me home to Bangor.

On reaching the house I was in a bit of pain, but I blamed Alan's driving skills for that. It was a great feeling to be with Becky and the boys, and as it happened, Dad was there too. After he went home we celebrated Siôn's birthday as a family.

Over the next few weeks I got a lot better and lived a fairly normal life. Steve, my stepbrother, was getting married to his girlfriend Tracey on 16 August – obviously, they'd been worried that I wouldn't be well enough to attend the wedding. I didn't feel one hundred percent that day to be honest and I'd been having pains, but I'd assumed that that was to be expected after the operation. As I tired easily Steve and Tracey had arranged a bedroom to be available for me to rest during the day. The wedding was a happy, joyous occasion, and it was lovely to be there with Becky, all my children and the rest of the family. Despite feeling weak and in a bit of pain at times, I coped fairly well during the day, and even managed to accompany Peredur, the best man, with his lemonade song during his speech!

Within a month of the operation, I started to feel a severe pain in my hips. I had to revert to taking painkillers, and started to worry that the bowel tumour was behind the pain as some time had passed since I'd had chemotherapy and radiotherapy. I made an appointment at Ysbyty Gwynedd with Dr Bale, who suggested that I should go and see the doctor who was responsible for the radiotherapy to see whether that could be linked to the pain. In the meantime, he arranged scans for me to assess whether anything else was amiss. The radiotherapy wasn't the cause, according to the doctor, and very soon I had another appointment to receive the results of the scan.

I remember sitting alone in the Alaw ward waiting room one morning in mid September 2014. Becky couldn't be there with me because Ianto was ill, but I wasn't expecting bad news as Mr Malik in Liverpool had reported that the liver operation had been successful. I was still waiting for bowel surgery in

Bangor, so it was natural for me to feel that the cause of the pain lay there, as that tumour was still in the bowel.

I saw Dr Fuller rather than Dr Bale that day – I knew Dr Fuller from my time as a trainee nurse, when she was a young medic. She had now become a cancer specialist. Dr Fuller spent some time explaining the results of the scan, and was evidently concerned as she told me the news. I was terribly shocked when she explained that seven new tumours had appeared on the liver. Of course, this explained all the pain. She showed me the scan, saying that the tumours had spread along the liver, and that they were inoperable. She explained that I would have to start a different course of chemotherapy to control the tumours, but eradicating the cancer was no longer an option. I started crying there and then, in her office, for what appeared to me a very long time. She was very kind, giving me plenty of time to pull myself together and to discuss how I was going to break the news to the rest of the family. She asked me to sit in the waiting room while she arranged a date for me to start chemotherapy, and I started crying again there. Eleri, one of the unit staff, came to move me to a private room and comforted me until I got the chemotherapy appointment letter.

I sat in the car for a good quarter of an hour, lost in thought, before setting off home to break the news to Becky. She only had to look at my face to realise that something was wrong. I started crying yet again as I told her that there was nothing more they could do to get rid of the cancer, and that I'd have to start another course of chemotherapy as no other treatment was viable. Obviously, Becky was shocked, bless her, and we both cried on each other's shoulders for a long time.

After we'd settled down, had a chat and a cup of tea, we made the decision that we would have to focus on being as positive as possible and enjoy life as much as we could. I spoke to Lisa and explained the situation to her, and asked her to support Lois, Owen and Beca. Dylan and Glenna came by shortly after hearing the news over the phone, and Mam and Clive came over too. Dad got a phone call and he was naturally devastated and tearful upon hearing the news.

I started a second course of chemotherapy very soon afterwards. This course required me to take intravenous medication through a fortnightly drip, and then to spend two days at home while a tennis-ball-sized sphere fed another drug into the vein. To secure access into my body I needed to have a PICC line insterted, which was a permanent pipeline into a vein in my arm. This saved me from having to have an injection in my hand every time I needed to give blood or take any direct intravenous medication. The only snag was that I had to keep it dry, so I couldn't go swimming with the boys and I had to take care in the shower. The medication had side-effects too. Although I wouldn't completely lose my hair it would possibly grow thinner. In the end, I didn't lose one hair from my head (although my hair did change colour) but I lost a lot of my body hair, which was an odd feeling as I'd always had such hairy legs. I needed to take a course of steroids for three days after taking the medication, and that affected me. Initially I had difficulty sleeping, but the biggest side-effect was the change in my personality. I was deliriously happy, full of myself and I'd spend money as if there was no tomorrow. I bought Becky a very expensive bag that she didn't really need, and I bought myself a lot of rugby shirts, until we realised what was going on and started keeping an eye on the situation!

'Would you be able to shave someone's head at the Urdd Eisteddfod in Bala?' That's how I came across Irfon for the first time. The question was asked by Kirsty Thompson from Awyr Las, when Irfon decided to shave his head and wear various wacky wigs in order to raise money for #Team Irfon.

When I met him for the first time I soon realised I was in the company of an unique personality. I'd met and known one other like him, someone I thought was unrivalled in the inspiration he gave me, and that was the late Bryan 'Yogi' Davies, a rugby player who suffered life-changing injuries. Both men, when someone would try to comfort them in their sad and hopeless situation, would end up emanating strength and positivity, and just being in their company could make someone feel better.

I see in Irfon – in his humour, his grace and positivity – strength, courage and stamina way beyond my capabilities, I suspect. I can only hope that we, the ones who know him and the ones who have come to know him during this tempestuous journey, can learn from him how to deal with life and all its challenges. He makes us appreciate what we have, to make the most of every opportunity and search for the best in people and situations instead of failing to see past the negative obstacles we face.

It is very rare for a rugby or football player to be named 'Man of the Match' in a game which is impossible to win, where the odds are spectacularly stacked up against him and where his opponents attack with ferocious force, skill and brutality. But believe you me, in this long and extremely cruel battle, Irfon Williams is 'Man of the Match'. We will remember and be proud of his passionate and unfailing performance, which will be a talking point amongst friends whilst we are all still in the game.

Rhys Meirion, Welsh opera singer

Chapter 6

#tîmirfon/#teamirfon

The #teamirfon activities were still taking place and keeping us very busy. Since starting the chemotherapy that September I'd been keen to carry on with the charity work – almost £40,000 had been raised by then. Becky and I organised a dinner and auction at Plas Rhianfa hotel on the Menai Straits for 30 September. Once again, just as with our wedding arrangements, the staff and managers were very kind and accommodating. Despite my worry that not many would come because the event was on a week night, all the tickets were sold out. The guest speaker for the evening was Scott Quinnell – he's a friend of John Burns, one of my friends – and he agreed to travel to north Wales with his wife, Nicola, and be the evening's guest speaker without charging a penny for his services. The weather was fantastic that night, and the guests were welcomed by talented harpist Dylan Cernyw playing in the background. He'd offered his services free of charge too, and succeeded in creating a lovely atmosphere. Everyone was relaxed and enjoying themselves. Of course, the wine was in full flow too, which helped encourage the spending!

Simon Jones, an auctioneer with the local firm Morgan Evans, was in charge of the auction again that night – and he was brilliant and up-beat. A number of people had donated items for the raffle and auction, and Becky and I had collected a number of items ourselves too. Robin McBryde had arranged some time before for the national team to sign a pile of rugby shirts for us – some of the shirts had gone in the evening held in memory of Arwyn, but there were some left, and some additional ones were donated by Robin and Scott. That evening succeeded in raising about five thousand pounds. One of the guests spent over £600 all by himself, and my friend Gary gave himself as an item in the auction too. He offered to be a slave for the day to whoever wanted him – £85 was paid for his services and my friends Huw and Siwsan got their money's worth, I'll bet!

In addition, a social evening was held at Maesgeirchen Social Club in September 2014 – neither Becky nor I really felt like going because we felt quite downhearted after the recent bad news, but I'm very glad we went because it was a great night. A group of lads were sponsored to wax their legs for the cause and there was another auction and bingo, along with entertainment by the local Tenovus Choir. It was a very colourful night!

Around that time, we received an invitation to attend an awards ceremony that was to be held in early October. Scottish Power, in partnership with the Trinity Mirror newspaper group, gives awards to community projects every year and #teamirfon had been nominated for a charity award. I was very glad to be at the George Hotel in Llandudno that night, as the awards were to be presented by Phil Bennett, the former Llanelli, Wales and Lions rugby player from the 1970s. The master of ceremonies was TV presenter Arfon Haines Davies, and it proved to be a great evening, full of laughter and emotion. Many of the guests had worked tirelessly in their communities throughout

With the Champion of Champions Award

north Wales, and were all fully deserving of public accolades. I was overjoyed when the charity award was won by #teamirfon, and proud of myself and everyone who had contributed to the campaign. A group of friends who'd been very active with #teamirfon were there with us that night, and Alan Owen and I, in particular, were absolutely thrilled to meet Phil Bennett. At the end of the ceremony Arfon Haines Davies announced that there was one more award to be presented: Community Champion. He said that this award was to be given to an individual who had worked tirelessly for the benefit of the community. As he listed that person's successes it became obvious that he was talking about me: he spoke about my enthusiasm for children's mental health, my role as a children's football and rugby coach, and of course #teamirfon. This came as quite a shock, and I found it impossible not to cry. I walked up to the stage wiping my tears away.

The press and media gave #teamirfon even more attention after that, and the same was true on social media. Local papers were tremendously supportive and the *Heno* programme on S4C was always willing to promote our activities. I was starting to get used to TV and radio interviews, and one standout experience was my interview with Beti George for her radio programme *Beti a'i Phobl* in December 2014. I was familiar with Beti George as she was a television newsreader when I was growing up, and her weekly interview programme – in which she interviews celebrities, or people who have made some sort of public contribution – is very popular. I understood that she is always very keen to have a private talk with her guests before recording each programme, and it was a privilege to have a chat with her beforehand. She's a really friendly lady who made me feel at ease in her company, exactly as I'd imagined she would be. The radio interview was successful and many people got in touch with me afterwards to praise it.

All the activities, and the attention they got in the press, served to raise awareness of bowel cancer and the plight of cancer patients, and more and more people were following my story and joining in the campaign. Groups of local schoolchildren started raising money through various activities, including pupils of Ysgol Brynrefail (a 24-hour radio show), Ysgol David Hughes (£1,287 was raised by a concert at the Anglesey Arms, Menai Bridge) and Ysgol Tryfan (who raised £580 by paying to not have to wear school uniform). This led to invitations to attend schools to receive cheques, which gave me an opportunity to thank them, and to speak publicly about cancer. I didn't expect such a positive response. I remember a message from one fifteen-year-old girl called Cara, who wanted to shave her head on her sixteenth birthday in memory of her auntie. On her birthday I met her and her family outside a hairdresser's in Bangor. Within minutes her beautiful long blonde hair was gone. Her family were very proud of her and very emotional – it was a really brave thing for such a young girl to have done.

Children surprised me more than anyone, to be honest. They would turn up at the door at random with bags of money for the cause, which they'd collected by selling cakes and so on. One girl had given up eating sweets for a fortnight to raise money, another had made hundreds of loom band bracelets to be sold and another group of local children had created a 'guess the teddy's name' game at their school's Christmas fair. The organiser of a Majorettes team in Llangefni had raised money, and I was invited there to watch them perform before they presented their cheque to #teamirfon. A nursery in Anglesey had raised money for the cause too, and I visited them with Nel Del, the Awyr Las mascot. I tried to accept every invitation to attend activities that were fundraising for #teamirfon – after all, they were working hard for a cause that I'd spotlighted – but I sometimes struggled to go as I felt very tired. Becky would tell me to slow down and take it easy, but I didn't always listen to her advice.

I was invited by the estate agent Dafydd Hardy to be a guest at the opening of his new office in Bangor, and he gave me the honour of officially declaring the office open! He told me it was because I was well-known in the area and was (in his words) an inspiration.

In December a community group in Bangor was organising a Christmas celebration in the high street. Becky organised a Santa Run from Bangor city centre down to Hirael and back; one mile in all. It proved very popular with over a hundred adults and children registering to run. By now #teamirfon had raised £50,000.

The Christmas celebration's organiser, Nigel Pickavance, was very supportive of the campaign, and organised a fun day in the Maesgeirchen area of Bangor as well as coordinating an

attempt to collect special tokens from the local regional nwspaper, the *Daily Post*, in order to win a prize for the charity. Nigel was the man behind the resurrection of the carnival in Bangor; and Samantha, one of Becky's school friends, who was responsible for arranging a carnival queens' competition, donated all proceeds (£605) to #teamirfon.

During the same period I was invited to the Betsi Cadwaladr Health Board awards evening. #teamirfon had been nominated for an award for charity work, and as so many people from the Health Board had also raised money, many of

Lois and I in 2014

them attended the evening with me. The award was won by #teamirfon and I was pleased that everyone's hard work and enthusiasm had been recognised.

The treatment was continuing, of course. I visited the Alaw unit every fortnight for chemotherapy, and was coping fairly well with the treatment and the PICC line in my arm.

Becky and I had discussed seeking a second opinion at The Christie, the specialist cancer hospital in Manchester. Initially I was reluctant to do this – I didn't want to stir up trouble, and I was very happy with the excellent care I was getting on Alaw. One day, while I was having my treatment, Becky went to discuss the matter with Dr Bale, who was more than willing to refer me there for a second opinion. It turned out that it wasn't unusual for north Wales patients to be seen at The Christie. Soon afterwards we received an appointment to see a bowel cancer specialist there.

Getting to The Christie from Bangor was fairly straightforward apart from the substantial increase in traffic as we approached Manchester. After parking in a multi-storey, Becky and I walked the hundred yards to the hospital entrance. I found it hard to assess the size of the hospital from the outside as it was in a busy area on the city outskirts and surrounded by a load of other buildings, but on walking into the busy entrance hall it was evident that it was enormous, and it was scarcely believable that such an enormous hospital existed solely to treat cancer patients. The word 'cancer' was visible everywhere, and that made things more real, somehow. As we walked down the corridor hand in hand a little boy ran towards us – his head was completely bald. Becky and I looked at each other. If that little lad could face cancer with a smile on his face, I could do it too. That little incident put everything into perspective – I thanked God that it was me, and not the children, going through this.

We found the outpatients department which was a vast place, and the waiting room was like a busy station full of all kinds of people of all ages. Usually, I was the youngest in the waiting rooms of cancer wards and units in north Wales, but here there were lots of children and young people. I started wondering what kind of cancer everyone had, and whether anyone was in the same situation as I was.

They have a very methodical system in The Christie, and I was sent immediately to have blood taken after registration. Thanks to the PICC line, this was a simple procedure. Then, I sat in the waiting room and waited for my name to be called – to make things easier for patients there was a TV screen in every waiting room giving regular updates on the clinic's progress – that is, how much waiting time to expect. Sadly, from my experience in every hospital, most clinics run at least an hour late, but at least this information made the waiting a little easier. There was information too about the kinds of services available, regarding issues such as welfare, mental health, social and financial matters. Becky and I decided that we wanted #teamirfon to support that kind of provision in Bangor.

The doctor I saw was called Dr Saifee Mullamitha, and he was a very nice man. He'd received all my history from Dr Bale and he listened closely to my story. He explained that he would treat me in exactly the same way as Dr Bale, but that he would include a drug which he called a biological agent. He also mentioned the possibility of my taking part in a clinical trial – that is, research trialling new treatments on patients. He didn't have one in mind at the time, but he would consider me if something suitable cropped up. He said that he wouldn't arrange to see me again, but that we were welcome to contact his secretary directly should I feel that I wanted to see him in the future. His explanation had given us faith in the care I was receiving in Bangor, but we were keen to discuss that biological agent with Dr Bale.

As I saw Dr Bale every fortnight prior to receiving the chemotherapy, the opportunity to talk about it came quite quickly. She explained that the treatment wasn't used in Wales, and that, as my blood tests showed that I appeared to be responding to the chemo, there wasn't much point considering it. I accepted that explanation without giving it too much more thought.

By the end of November 2014 it was time for me to have another scan to measure the tumours – especially those on the liver. My blood levels had been fairly stable, and the hope was that the tumours would have reduced sufficiently to allow me to have further surgery. As usual, waiting for the results was hard, and Becky and I were obviously on tenterhooks in the waiting room. The news that awaited us was bad and unexpected – the tumours hadn't shrunk at all and one or two had even grown in size, the biggest now measuring 8cm in length. We had a tearful talk with Dr Bale about the implications of this news, and she said that there was no longer any hope that treatment would succeed in getting rid of the cancer. Breaking that news to our family and friends was hard.

On 18 December we saw Mr Malik in Liverpool. He too was obviously disappointed with the results and confirmed that I couldn't be offered liver surgery as things stood. He also spoke about the biological agent we'd been told about at The Christie, and he named a drug called Cetuximab. He told us that many of his patients had experienced good results with this drug, but that, as he understood it, it wasn't available in Wales. Becky and I felt quite confused after that appointment – of course, we didn't understand the politics, the policies and so on, that were responsible for this situation. Becky was really upset, and she called Dr Bale from the car park in Liverpool to say that we were anxious to try this drug, Cetuximab. Dr Bale was adamant that it was unavailable in Wales, and her advice to us was to go home and have a good Christmas.

We were both aware of a system called IPFR, or Individual Patient Funding Request – a policy established by the Welsh Government to enable health boards to apply for non-mainstream funding. Every health board has a multidisciplinary panel that hears the applications and decides on the validity of the request ... but we didn't appreciate at the time how difficult it was to navigate that system. We were quite naïve, thinking that the health board would be sure to support the request for me to be allowed to receive the drug. Dr Bale's opinion wasn't so encouraging, as she had never been successful with a request to the panel, and although she explained that she wasn't hopeful for a positive feedback from the IPFR panel she agreed to support the application for funding for the treatment.

The application was made straight away. Becky contacted our Welsh Assembly Member, Alun Ffred Jones, who managed to persuade the panel to meet earlier, on Christmas Eve rather than 20 January.

By then I was back at work which gave me a different kind of focus. Yvonne, my manager, was still really supportive, and I was enjoying working and keeping busy. My colleagues were very supportive too, and although I couldn't carry out all my duties (I didn't travel to meetings in Wrexham, for example) I felt that I was still able to make a difference by supporting other team members and finishing bits of work that had been left in limbo since I'd been taken ill.

On Christmas Eve I was in my car having attended a meeting in Caernarfon. I received a phone call from a member of the IPFR panel explaining that my application for them to finance the Cetuximab drug had been turned down. Although disappointed, I wasn't surprised by the decision. He explained that I had three options. Firstly, I could appeal against the decision with Dr Bale's support; secondly, I could investigate the possibilities of financing the drug myself; or thirdly – and I was quite shocked when he suggested this – I could move to England to receive the drug there. I asked him for the paperwork involving the case, including the panel meeting minutes, and he agreed to send them to me.

It had been a time of enormous stress. That night, Becky and I decided to put everything aside for a short while in order to focus on enjoying Christmas the following day – after all, the two little ones had no idea what was going on. We had loads of things to do, and after spending hours wrapping Christmas presents, Becky went to bed leaving me to wrap the last few. I cried that night on my own, entertaining all kinds of morbid thoughts. Would this be my last Christmas? Was my life that worthless seeing that the NHS refused to fund treatment to save it? All these things were at the back of our minds throughout Christmas, and we were anxious to receive the IPFR panel's papers as soon as possible in order to appeal against the decision. We managed to enjoy Christmas – there were thirteen of us celebrating together, and although everyone was aware of the situation, no-one uttered the C-word all day.

When the dust settled, Becky was obviously determined to find answers and alternative possibilities. The panel's documents had arrived and I remember sitting at the dining-room table going through the papers not knowing where or how to start responding to the panel's decision. For the first time since the diagnosis we felt bereft of hope. I heard of a woman who'd been through a similar situation with her mother, and she put us in touch with a bowel cancer specialist in London. I sometimes woke up in the middle of the night to find that Becky was awake, and doing some research on the ipad – within no time she'd learnt a great deal about that specialist at Hammersmith hospital. His name was Dr Wassan, a bowel cancer specialist who also led research in the UK involving the cancer and the Cetuximab drug. Becky arranged a private appointment for us with him in London, and my GP sent him information about my case beforehand.

My treatment was ongoing throughout all this, and although Dr Bale had agreed to support the appeal she was negative about the likely result as there was no new evidence to submit to the panel. One reason why I had been refused the drug was a piece of research that NICE (the National Institute of Clinical Excellence) had approved. Becky and I were familiar with NICE, a body that collects research about all kinds of diseases and suggests the best ways to treat any kind of illness on the basis of that research, as we both used its findings in our everyday work. NICE had published a piece of research which suggested that a high percentage of patients who were given Cetuximab with the oxyplatin chemotherapy died following surgery. Of course, being accustomed to reading research papers we didn't accept that this research was relevant to me, as I was now getting the Irinotecan chemo (which was a different drug). Even so, Dr Bale strongly suspected that any cancer specialist would be very wary of suggesting Cetuximab followed by surgery –it was considered to be a drug that prolonged patients' lives rather than a drug to reduce tumours to prepare for surgery to eliminate the disease.

Later in January 2015 Becky and I travelled to London. The appointment was late in the day and the journey by train and underground to reach Hammersmith Hospital was a long one. Dr Wassan was a nice man, and he took his time discussing my case. He explained that the recent research was quite inconclusive, and that it was likely to be withdrawn by NICE as many cancer doctors, like Dr Bale, were concerned about a negative outcome for their patients. Dr Wassan also explained that genetic tests were carried out on bowel cancer patients – tests to discover whether their particular type of cancer was likely to respond to a biological agent like Cetuximab. The main test was named K-RAS, and he invited me to take part in research carried out in London that would discover whether my K-RAS result was positive. That would involve moving to London for a period, and registering with a GP there. I left the appointment in a much more hopeful frame of mind, and after Becky and I discussed the difficulties of moving to London, we decided that that was what I would do, if necessary. Within half an hour Becky had contacted her cousin, Emma, in Richmond, who was more than willing for me to stay with her and her husband for a period to receive the treatment. It felt good to be able to phone the family with good news, for once.

Travelling on the underground we both had smiles on our faces and a feeling of relief came over us. It was easy to enjoy *Billy Elliot* that evening, and a have a good night's sleep in our hotel. During the return train journey to Bangor the next morning Becky was at it again on her ipad researching the genetic tests. She spoke to the national laboratory in Cardiff, which serves the whole of Wales, and got confirmation that the

In London

K-RAS test was available there. Becky started communicating with a member of the IPFR panel about these tests as we felt that a positive test result would comprise new additional information that could be submitted to the panel. Becky contacted Claire Burston at Aintree directly to see whether a sample of the tumour that was taken out of the liver the previous August could be sent to be tested as no samples were available from the original colonoscopy, and we received confirmation that it would be possible to do that. The team at Aintree made arrangements to carry out the test.

Neither Becky nor I were working by then – Becky's life was centred on researching treatments, collecting information and so on, while I tried to focus on keeping healthy in order to be in a strong situation to fight the cancer. I arranged to speak to one of the senior pharmacists at Ysbyty Gwynedd – I explained my situation to her and she set about collecting information for me about the costs and availability of Cetuximab should I decide to fund the treatment myself. It was possible to get a supply of the drug to the hospital in a day, so that was no problem – but the cost for three months was £15,000, far more than most of the drugs provided by the NHS. That was just the cost of the drug, and had I not been already receiving treatment from the NHS, then nursing costs and so on would have incurred additional expense.

By the February half-term break we were informed that the appeal had been rejected. This wasn't a shock, but by this time we were determined to battle against the system which appeared unfair and impenetrable to patients and their families.

After thinking carefully, Becky and I decided to announce on Facebook what had happened. Becky wrote a public post on her page that evening, 18 February, 2015:

Today Irfon for the second time was declined a drug that

he needs to have a fighting chance at beating his Cancer. The Welsh NHS which is supposed to be there to preserve life is denying Irfon a chance of cure. It has been a desperate, degrading and unbelievably stressful 8 weeks appealing for a drug, a drug that will not be prescribed due to cost. To obtain the medication Irfon will now have to move to England – receive his care away from family and many friends and away from his Welsh language. Irfon has received excellent nursing care locally which we have valued, however the postcode lottery is a disgrace and Welsh Cancer patients are being treated by the Welsh Government as second class citizens.

The response we got was unexpected, to say the least, and the situation had obviously enraged many people in the community. There were calls for the money that #teamirfon had raised to be used to pay for the drug for me, and individuals started questioning why that wasn't possible. Kirsty at Awyr Las had to explain that we had raised all that money for other purposes, not to fund the treatment of individual patients. Some said that this was a disgrace, especially bearing in mind how much money #teamirfon had raised, making comments like, 'and with you having worked for the health board so long yourself!'. More than one person suggested that a new campaign would have to be started to finance the treatment, and one colleague of mine set up a fundraising page and advertised it on Facebook, urging people to donate money. I had to contact her quite quickly and ask her to delete it, although I was very grateful for her support and enthusiasm.

It was important that we calmed the waters quickly before matters got out of hand, so that Becky and I could deal with the issue with dignity. Although I didn't object to the practice of raising money for individuals in need, I wasn't comfortable with doing that personally. It didn't seem fair to me. I was also adamant that the #teamirfon money shouldn't be used on me – that money was intended to help cancer patients in north Wales through Awyr Las. People were obviously angry at the health board for refusing me the treatment, but in truth this was a political matter as it's the government that is responsible for financing health services, and IPFR is their policy.

We got a lot of press attention, locally and nationally, and as well as speaking to the media and papers in Wales I did interviews for the BBC network and for the *Daily Mail*, who came to the house to interview me.

Becky and I felt terribly stressed, frustrated and worthless. I'm a very proud Welshman and I felt that the country I loved and felt allegiance to was letting me down. I thought of all the other patients who hadn't had this drug – maybe they weren't aware of it, or maybe they lacked the confidence to challenge the system, to question doctors and politicians. How many people had died sooner than necessary because of this policy? I felt strongly that I had a responsibility to raise awareness and challenge this terribly unfair system … but first, I had to deal with my own situation.

Another appointment was arranged for me at The Christie with Dr Mullamitha. He fully sympathised and felt just as frustrated as I did about the situation in Wales with regard to Cetuximab. He'd seen many successes as a result of the treatment – not all patients responded well to the drug and some didn't even respond well enough to qualify for surgery, but at least they lived longer after Cetuximab had reduced the tumours. He felt that there was roughly a 15% chance that I'd get rid of the cancer completely if the treatment was successful. That gave me a bit of a boost. Dr Mullamitha agreed to treat me with Cetuximab at The Christie as he was able to access the drug through the Cancer Drugs Fund (CDF), but I'd have to live in England, and have a GP there.

Sarah, Becky's cousin, was a nurse in Chester and lived in Ellesmere Port, and she very kindly offered me a room in her house for the duration of the treatment at The Christie. Although it went against the grain to some extent – I felt strongly that neither I nor anyone else should have to move across the border to get treatment – this drug could possibly save my life, or at least keep me alive for longer. I had no choice, in reality. The opportunity was too good to miss, and I registered with a GP in Ellesmere Port and prepared to spend quite a lot of time there.

It is devastating enough to be diagnosed with cancer at any time of life – but when you are young, at the height of your career and with young children, the moment can be life changing. How you react will, from my experience as a GP for 34 years, shape the future.

Irfon accepted the diagnosis and immediately looked at the positive. How was he going to manage the rest of his life? As a Mental Health worker with an interest in mindfulness, he decided his glass was to be half full and embarked on a mission to help himself and others in the same situation, embracing the public and media to highlight the need for positive action in cancer.

At a time of greatest need and susceptibility, he came up to a brick wall. The drug that could help him was not available in his native land. It was not the first time I had suggested to a patient that, in order to receive the treatment, re-location would be required. Against his principles, but to prolong his life, he moved across the border to England, where the drug was available, and was successful in curtailing the cancer. He would not have survived more than a few months without it – now, three years on, although not cured, he is writing of his journey.

Positive thoughts and positive attitude undoubtedly make the path easier; it gives a feeling of 'doing something' and it makes caring for patients with cancer a more seamless process for the professionals, family and friends.

Irfon has been remarkable and with the help of Becky, has been able to reach the goals he set at the onset. With his diary, his journey will be shared by many for years to come and the name Irfon Williams will be synonymous with a positive attitude to a devastating disease.

Dr David Jones, GP

Chapter 7

Hawl i Fyw / Fighting Chance

Very soon, the news spread that I was moving to England to get treatment. Becky and a group of our close friends felt very strongly that they should raise awareness of the injustice, and as they discussed starting a campaign Aled Prys Davies, one of our closest friends, came up with the name 'Hawl i Fyw' or 'Fighting Chance' in English. A public page was set up on Facebook at the end of February 2015 and within a fortnight over 24,000 people had responded and joined the group.

That February was a very busy month. As the media were showing so much of an interest in the story I had to be very sure of the facts when discussing my health as well as the political issues that affected the policies which stated that I couldn't receive Cetuximab in Wales. We also had to take care to ensure that I was speaking from my own viewpoint as a patient, and Becky as a patient's wife, rather than from the viewpoint of NHS staff.

I was invited to talk live on Welsh language radio and BBC Wales as well as the *Newyddion 9* news programme on TV, which was a very challenging experience, where I had to remind the host, Rhodri Llywelyn, that I was a patient, not a politician. Nevertheless, I was sure of my facts and was quite realistic in accepting that ensuring full access to all treatments for everyone was impossible, there being no bottomless pot of money. Newspapers, especially the *Daily Post*, reported on the story regularly, and the local papers, of course, were very supportive and a great help in raising awareness.

Alun Ffred Jones, the Plaid Cymru Assembly Member for Arfon, was very supportive and Becky and I were invited to meet him, Hywel Williams MP and Elin Jones, the Assembly Member for Ceredigion, at the Plaid Cymru Conference in Caernarfon on 7 March 2015. The meeting was a very useful one, and Plaid offered not only to support me as an individual but also the family, and the campaign as well. It was important to us from the outset that this political issue was above any specific party, and we called for cross-party backing. Andrew R. T. Davies, the Conservative Assembly Member, was positive too. He agreed to meet us to discuss the case further and offer his support. The Liberal Democrats didn't respond to any of our invitations, and the Labour Party were very reluctant to speak to us. Of course, we'd written to Mark Drakeford, the Health Minister at the time, and his letter of reply didn't make much sense, to put it mildly.

I was gobsmacked while I watched the live TV broadcast from the Senedd one day, a few weeks later. I heard Leanne

Hywel Williams, Leanne Wood and Dafydd Wigley
from Plaid Cymru supporting #FightingChance

Wood, the Plaid Cymru leader, interrogate Carwyn Jones about the matter, urging him to meet me to discuss the case. His response was not encouraging, as he stated publicly that he couldn't see any benefit in that kind of meeting, describing me as an 'unfortunate case'. I was even more gobsmacked some time after that while watching *Prime Minister's Question Time* from Westminster. Hywel Williams MP had raised the matter there and it was strange to hear David Cameron, the Prime Minister at the time, talk about me and say that he really hoped that I would get access to the treatment I needed in England, although he felt it was a disgrace that the treatment wasn't available to me in Wales.

All the attention my case was getting was great for the campaign, and I started to receive countless messages describing a great number of cases similar to mine. These gave me the necessary impetus to carry on campaigning. I began to feel angry when I considered how many people had died unnecessarily or prematurely, without having had a fair deal and access to a treatment that would have benefited them.

Graham Satchell from BBC Breakfast came with his cameraman to our house, and they were keen to film us with the children for a news item on the campaign. I'd asked Lois to come over too but as she was older they didn't want to film her – they only wanted the 'cute' little boys. Well, I was quite miffed about this, but Lois was understanding, fair play to her. I was determined to include Lois, Owen and Beca in the campaign as much as possible, and made a point of referring to myself as a father of five children in every report and interview. Yes, Graham got his 'cute factor' during the filming as Siôn announced at the end of the piece that he loved me 'all the way to God'.

A committee had to be formed for Hawl i Fyw/Fighting Chance, and it was decided to hold a public meeting in Bangor for this purpose. A lot of ideas sprang up from that meeting, and lots of people offered their support. Ultimately, the committee was established under Becky's leadership, with our friends Dr Liz Whitehead (who was also a colleague of mine), Sue Roberts, Aled Prys Davies and Dyfed Jones from Llanfairpwll (who also felt very strongly about the cause due to personal reasons) as members. A little later Patrick Roberts, who had been so supportive of us by virtue of his position with Awyr Las, joined the committee too. We were terribly disappointed when we heard that some of our friends, who worked for Betsi Cadwaladr Health Board, couldn't publicly and naturally offer us their support due to our work. I heard that an email had been circulated around the Board warning people to be careful about supporting a political campaign, especially on social media – and there was little doubt they were referring to Hawl i Fyw/Fighting Chance. It turned out that local county council staff had also been sent the same warning. Aled Prys worked for Ynys Môn Council, and Liz (as well as Becky and I) was employed by the NHS. I contacted the Royal College of Nursing for advice in order to avoid any professional problem: as long as I kept my professional life out of it entirely, they said, it shouldn't be a problem. Becky was given the same advice. It was important to remember that in the context of the campaign I was a patient, although some people found it difficult to differentiate between my professional role and my personal life with regard to Hawl i Fyw/Fighting Chance. And so it began – the committee worked tirelessly behind the scenes, as it were, supporting Becky and myself who were the public faces of all the activity.

From then on, the campaign grew bigger than anyone could have imagined. We received assistance from numerous local businesses, and construction firm Watkin Jones of Bangor, together with Stephen Edwards' broadcasting and media production company Cread Cyf, were very good to us, offering their services free of charge to develop a logo for the campaign and produce posters and forms to promote the process. Obviously our greatest support was in north Wales, but messages of support came from people throughout Wales, Britain and all over the world. It was quite frightening in one way, and I had to grow accustomed to the publicity very quickly. Of course, it was important that we maintained a distance between the work of #teamirfon and Awyr Las, a charity affiliated with the Health Board, and the Hawl i Fyw/Fighting Chance campaign. We regularly tried to explain the difference – Hawl i Fyw wasn't a charity, but a campaign to change attitudes, raise awareness and, if possible, influence Government policy. I felt very strongly that I wanted to carry on raising money for Alaw ward, because the intention from the very beginning was to ease the lives of local cancer sufferers. The political problem, in my opinion, didn't change that at all.

Meanwhile, I had my treatment to focus on. In order to register with a GP in the Ellesmere Port area I had to present two utility bills from my temporary home showing my name and address on them. Sarah, Becky's cousin, had to add me to her domestic council tax account – meaning that she lost her single person's discount. It all took some time to arrange, and after all that was sorted I had to make an appointment with my new GP. I remember walking into the surgery feeling like a naughty schoolboy cheating the system, and I had no idea what sort of response I'd get from Dr Hogan, my new GP. But I needn't have worried – Dr Hogan was very understanding and had encountered many people who had done the same thing before me.

Even so, I was very nervous during that first journey to Sarah's house in Ellesmere Port, to stay the night before going for treatment to The Christie. I was given blood tests to ensure that everything was in order – unfortunately, after working myself up to receive the drug the treatment had to be postponed because I had a high temperature. A week later, off we went on the same journey again. It was very hard to leave Bangor – we'd arranged for Mam and Clive to look after the boys, after trying to explain to them that Mam and Dad were going away for a few days so that Dad could get his special medicine. I was sad that this kind of thing was going to be part of their lives for months, and felt strongly that they needed the stability of having their parents around more than ever during such a turbulent period. But children are very resilient, and they both looked at going to stay with Nain and Taid as an adventure and a pleasure, and I knew they were sure to get spoilt rotten.

After arriving at The Christie on the morning of 18 March 2015, and having my blood taken once again, I had to wait to see Dr Mullamitha, who prepared me for the chemotherapy and Cetuximab that I was to receive that afternoon. He explained the side-effects once again – but to be quite honest, I didn't care about them at all, I just felt really happy that I was there at last to receive the treatment, three months after hearing about the drug for the first time. I had to wait hours before the treatment commenced that day because the pharmacy couldn't release the drug until they got the results of the blood tests. It was about 3 p.m. by the time I was called in to the day unit. I was introduced to two or three of the nurses, who were very nice and obviously aware of my story. Unfortunately, one nurse found that my temperature was slightly higher than it should be and we had to wait for Dr Mullamitha to give the go-ahead to carry on with the treatment. Having had a look at it, he was confident that the temperature was caused by the cancer itself, and not an infection. It was an incredible feeling to see the liquid-filled bag go up on the drip stand – at last, I was about to get the drug I'd been dreaming about for so long.

It was after midnight by the time everything was over, and the day unit was supposed to close at eight! Two very nice nurses had agreed to work late to look after me, and it goes without saying that I was on my knees by the time we started the journey back to Ellesmere Port.

Two days later I had to return to The Christie to have the chemo pump removed before travelling back to Bangor to see the boys. I realised that the treatment would be quite challenging and would obviously tire me, and Becky of course. I was extremely grateful that Dr Mullamitha had anticipated the strain that the situation would cause and had decided to give me a double dose of Cetuximab every fortnight with the chemo rather than the usual weekly dose. This meant that I'd get to spend more time at home in between treatments.

It felt good to be home in Bangor after that first treatment, and knowing that the process was in motion was a major relief. Although I didn't know it at the time, Becky was starting to worry that I wasn't showing any sign of developing the drug's side-effects. After reading up on the topic and discussing it with Dr Mullamitha and the nurses, it was clear that an acne-type rash was a good sign that the body was responding well to the drug. She needn't have worried – I woke up a week after the first treatment feeling quite different. My face and head were swollen up and plastered in spots, especially around my nose, forehead and neck ... very painful, terribly itchy spots. I remember looking in the mirror incredulously. I'd avoided acne in my teens so now my mates had a great opportunity to tease me. I sent a selfie to Lois, and got a message back from her calling me 'pizza face'! After about three days I'd got used to my appearance and by the weekend I was ready to go out for the first time. When we arrived at our friends Aled and Gwawr's house, I realised that Becky had given them advance warning. Fair play, their reaction was supportive. Of course, despite the discomfort, pain and serious itching, I also celebrated the rash's appearance because it was a sign that the Cetuximab was doing its job. It got worse, and as the treatment went on, the rash spread to the rest of my head, over my chest, back and legs, and everywhere itched terribly. I was given medication to partly relieve the symptoms, but I got used to it in the end (although I tended to go out to the cinema and similar places where people couldn't see me). Every time I saw Dr Mullamitha he'd be thrilled, celebrating the fact that the rash was so angry!

I experienced other side-effects too – including one very unusual one. My eyelashes grew long, and started curling up. Becky was quite jealous, saying that women paid a fortune for that look. I had to trim them once or twice as they rubbed against my glasses!

The second treatment a fortnight later ran late too, and it was past midnight when we got back to Ellesmere Port. Once again, we had to travel back to The Christie two days later to have the pump removed and the PICC line treated. It was all quite exhausting, and Becky decided to look at other possibilities. She contacted various friends of mine and soon plenty of them had offered to help, taking time off work and so on to take me to The Christie directly from Bangor every fortnight – a 200 mile round trip – to avoid having to stay in Ellesmere Port all the time. After discussing it with Manon and the staff in the Alaw unit, they agreed to remove the pump and treat the PICC so that I didn't have to return to The Christie to get that done.

During this period, the advice of our GP in Bangor was really helpful. Although I was officially registered in England, Dr David Jones could treat me as a local visitor while I was at home with my family. The situation was ridiculous really, but I was extremely grateful to Dr Jones and the Alaw ward staff for agreeing to do this, which meant that the rest of the treatment in Manchester would be easier from then on.

While I was dealing with this, the campaign was getting

stronger. I remember my friend Robin McBryde talking about me on *Heno* on S4C, and declaring his support for Hawl i Fyw/Fighting Chance. T-shirts were printed by the Krypton Cloth company in Bangor, who were very generous – Robin had asked us to send him some and it was fantastic to see the Wales national rugby team support the campaign by wearing Hawl i Fyw/Fighting Chance T-shirts before their six nations match against Italy that year. Every squad member agreed to be photographed holding a Hawl i Fyw/Fighting Chance poster to show their support. Local sports clubs like Bangor Rugby Club

My mate, Robin McBryde, showing his support

and Cae Glyn Football Club in Caernarfon wore shirts bearing the words #teamirfon and #HawliFyw, and many clubs sent photos of their teams displaying posters supporting the campaign. A number of sponsored bike rides were held too – Andy Owen and about fifteen friends cycled to Cardiff and raised a substantial sum of money. John Burns and four of his mates cycled from Lands End to John o' Groats to raise money for The Christie Hospital, and dozens of people ran races regularly to raise money for #teamirfon.

Aled Prys had been thinking about projects to raise awareness, and had contacted the singer Elin Fflur and Mari Pritchard, a renowned musician and choir conductor who does a lot to develop young musical talent in Anglesey, about an idea he had.

I knew them both, and considered them very talented and very nice people too. Mari's husband Gary and I were members of the social branch of the Beaumaris brass band, called LSW (Last of the Summer Wind!), and enjoying the experience. A meeting was arranged to discuss the idea – namely the possibility of recording a famous Welsh song for the benefit of the campaign, at Sain studios near Caernarfon. The song choice was an obvious one: 'Hawl i Fyw' by the popular Welsh singer and politician Dafydd Iwan. We all got together – Elin, Mari, the studio manager, Aled, Dyfed and me ... and the man himself, Dafydd Iwan! Mari and Elin were keen to bring some of Wales' leading singers together, Band Aid style, to sing the song in order to draw attention to the political system of access to treatment that wasn't fair to all – a great idea, but quite a challenge. I didn't realise at the time what an impact this project would have, both on me as an individual and on the Welsh public.

There was no stopping Mari and Elin and soon they had a lengthy list of Wales' most popular singers and musicians who

Recording 'Hawl i Fyw' in Sain recording studio

had volunteered their time, and specific recording dates had been booked. Becky and I were very keen to arrange a holiday for the four of us when the opportunity arose, and as Mam and Clive were spending Easter that year at their home in France, we decided to take the opportunity to spend a week there with them. My stepbrother, Steve, and his family were going to travel there from their home in Brussels too. Unfortunately, that meant that I couldn't be at the studio to see the song being recorded. But in a way, I was glad too, because I'm sure I would have found it hard to cope with what was sure to be an emotional day.

The third treatment at The Christie went very smoothly. My friend John Burns had been given the task of taking me that week, and I was so glad that I didn't have to stay in Ellesmere Port. John came to fetch me at 7 a.m. in order to get to The Christie by 9.30 – he'd taken a day off work, explaining to his colleagues that he was taking me for treatment. John and I had

A poster showing the support of the Welsh national rugby squad

fun that day, laughing and reminiscing about the old days in the rugby club and generally putting the world to rights. I had to tell him to calm down once or twice in case our laughter was annoying some of the other patients who maybe didn't feel as good as I did.

By now, ITV had arranged to produce two TV documentaries about me: *Y Byd ar Bedwar* for S4C in Welsh and *Wales This Week* in English on ITV. Siân Morgan Lloyd, the TV presenter, wanted to follow me around at home in Bangor, in Ellesmere Port and at The Christie. The Christie Hospital communications department was very supportive and willing to facilitate the filming as much as possible, and Dr Mullamitha was aso happy to take part in the programme. When I went there for the fourth treatment, Siân Morgan Lloyd and a cameraman followed me. The communications officer spent the day with us telling us what we could and could not film: she was astonished that an entire programme was going to be produced in Welsh, and showed a great interest in the language. Her face was a picture as we sat in the waiting room – a Chinese family was sat on the opposite side of the waiting room, and one of them, quite a young man, got up and walked towards me. He shook my hand, and said in Welsh, 'Irfon Williams, ia? Hawl i Fyw? Dwi'n dilyn chdi ar Facebook!' ('I follow you on Facebook!'). The poor communication officer's jaw nearly hit the floor. It turned out that the man had spent his childhood in the Llanberis area with his family, who ran the Chinese takeaway, and had received his education at Ysgol Brynrefail, Llanrug, before moving back to Manchester.

That week, I was halfway through the Cetuximab treatment, and awaiting the results of a blood test that shows the cancer's activity and measures it through a certain protein in the blood. My levels had been fairly stable since having the second chemo, at around 60 to 80. I received brilliant news as

I got the treatment that week: the reading had halved and Dr Mullamitha strongly believed that this was a good sign, and that I was responding to the drug. Of course, he was also still celebrating the fact that my rash was still there.

Following that good news, we went off to France for a richly deserved holiday in the sun after such a busy, exhausting and stressful period. While we were there, the big day took place at Sain studios. I was in touch with Aled and Liz, and they both reported that there was a real buzz there. The Brythoniaid Male Voice Choir had been invited to join in, and as Dad was a member of the choir he'd had a bit of attention during the day, doing interviews for newspapers and television and so on. The *Heno* TV programme had recorded the day's events which were to be broadcast that week as a special programme. I had a chat with Dad, and it was obvious that he had found it difficult at times to hold back the tears while singing. For some reason, he'd found himself thinking quite a lot during the day about Arwyn, as well as about me. I won't name everyone who was part of that special day but I will be forever grateful to everyone who gave their time to the cause. Mari and Elin had worked tirelessly on the project and had produced something worthwhile. When I saw the video for the first time I was quite shocked, to be honest, to think that all those individuals had given up their time to support me and the campaign too. It was a privilege to see stars of the Welsh music scene there singing their parts; people like Dafydd Iwan, Bryn Fôn, Rhys Meirion, Yws Gwynedd, Alys Williams, Meinir Gwilym and of course Elin Fflur. It was a pleasure to hear my friend Bedwyr Morgan's duet with Sarah Louise, and of course, I was made up to see that Caryl Parry Jones was there, especially as I used to fancy her when I was younger!

The campaign went from strength to strength after that. All copies of the CD were sold out in no time, and I received regular messages from total strangers praising the campaign, and video clips of children singing the song. Becky and I were invited to visit Ysgol yr Hendre in Caernarfon for a fundraising event shortly after that. The welcome we got there was special, and as we went from class to class every child knew who I was, and nearly every one of them wanted to sing 'Hawl i Fyw'. The problem, of course, was that my eyes welled up every time I heard the song, as they still do to this day.

There was great activity on the Hawl i Fyw/Fighting Chance Facebook page as people posted photos of themselves with campaign posters and so on. They included the great and good, and it was really exciting when messages and photos were received from members of the Wales football squad, especially Gareth Bale. Climber Gwyn Griffiths had sent a picture of himself in the Himalayas with a Hawl i Fyw/Fighting Chance

flag. But best of all was the picture posted by Allan Chambers, one of the group who had swum across the Menai Straits the previous year. He'd travelled to the North Pole with two former England international rugby players, Steve Borthwick and Lewis Moody, and they'd carried the Hawl i Fyw/Fighting Chance flag with them all the way to be planted in the pole. I never imagined I'd be so grateful to two England rugby players! But all this conveyed a strong message about the strength of the campaign, and it was now very difficult for anyone to ignore it.

Liverpool's Jamie Carragher supporting the cause

The politicians, especially Leanne Wood and the Conservative Andrew R. T. Davies, were continuing to put pressure on Welsh First Minister Carwyn Jones to meet Becky and I, and ultimately, he had no choice but to do so. We were a bit shocked to receive a call from one of his staff to arrange a meeting at the Government's Offices in Llandudno Junction in July 2015. Meanwhile, the treatment at The Christie was happening every fortnight, and my friends Robbie and Al Prys, and Dad, had kept me company during the long days and the post-midnight journeys back home to Bangor. The period between the treatment and the scans to measure its success was an anxious one, and on top of everything we had to decide whether we wanted to let the TV crew record Dr Mullamitha giving me the result. I remember discussing this with Becky on the way to Manchester that morning – that we had to accept whatever was ahead of us, but we were both very hopeful that we were going there to receive good news. The entire family was on tenterhooks all day, I'm sure, waiting for our call. Dr Mullamitha had kindly arranged with The Christie communications officer that he'd meet us in his office that day rather than in the outpatients' clinic, as we had a TV crew with us. It was a sunny day, the rash was itching, I was extremely nervous and Becky was quite tearful. Without beating around the bush, Dr Mullamitha presented the results – he was evidently very happy as he explained that the result was much better than he'd anticipated. The tumours in my body had reduced by 60%, which meant that I would certainly live longer. He warned us that he'd discussed my case in detail with a team of surgeons in Manchester, and that their response had not been positive – if I were a patient of theirs none of them would consider surgery because there were so many tumours which had spread all along the liver. That didn't worry me too much because I had faith in Mr Malik, who is an ambitious surgeon. I was confident that there was now a very strong possibility that Mr Malik would be willing to consider another operation.

Phoning around to share the news was a pleasure. I decided to post a statement on Facebook and I received hundreds of messages of congratulation. The treatment had been a difficult journey and Becky and I were very emotional that day, feeling relieved that the drug had worked after we'd battled so hard and been so resolute. To tell you the truth, I'd been worrying what people would have thought if the treatment hadn't been successful after all the fuss we'd made about getting access to Cetuximab, but in reality, I don't think many would have blamed me for following that path, whatever the result might have been. After that day, I was much more confident and adamant that I could beat this disease and live the life I'd hoped for, for myself, Becky and the children.

Despite my best efforts, carrying on working had proved impossible. My work friends had been behind me all the time, sending messages and enquiring about me. Yvonne, my manager, had been brilliant and more supportive than anyone could have expected, to be fair. But by now it was obvious that I needed to discuss my future at work. After an honest conversation, Becky and I came to the decision that the only sensible option for me was to take retirement due to ill health, and Yvonne was happy to support that choice. It was an enormous step to take, considering I was only 45 years old that July, a young man who was still passionate about my job and career, but in all honesty the decision was a much easier one than I'd expected. Being at home had given me an opportunity to assess the important things in life, and for me, my priority was to spend time with my family. Although I'd enjoyed my job, I recognised how much stress I'd been under during the years before I became ill and I didn't want to return to that. I needed to focus on my health and on getting better. Yvonne sorted everything out for me, helping me with the paperwork and supporting me throughout the whole process in a most considerate and compassionate way. I was going to retire in September 2015 and receive the NHS pension which I'd been paying into, thank goodness, since I was 18. Incidentally, I had to wait until the following year to have my retirement party, which was held in the Management Centre at Bangor University. Colleagues past and present had arranged a flashmob to the Bruno Mars song 'Uptown Funk', and I had a hell of a shock when Becky got up to join in as well! Unbeknown to me, she'd been practising for the event with them to give me a surprise.

Very soon I got an appointment to see Mr Malik at Aintree. His message was unequivocal: he was willing to offer me surgery, and was confident that he could succeed in eradicating the cancer from the liver. He explained that this would provide an opportunity to treat the bowel at the same time, and he'd arranged for me to meet his colleague, Mr Skaiff, the consultant surgeon who specialised in bowel treatments. Although the team in Bangor at the start of the journey had explained that I would need a permanent colostomy, Mr Skaiff didn't agree. He believed that the tumour could be treated by cutting away a section of the intestine with the tumours and reattaching the two ends back together. Both men explained that it would be a major operation – the liver would be dealt with first, then the bowel, and I would probably then need to spend a period in the intensive care unit following the surgery. Because of all the chemotherapy I'd received they would have to wait a while before carrying out the surgery, in order to let the body settle down and to make sure that I'd be able to recover properly. This obviously had me worried, but Mr Malik was confident that the tumours wouldn't grow back quickly and put a stop to the surgery. Dr Mullamitha agreed to treat me with two further courses of Cetuximab without the chemo in order to keep things stable. In the meantime there was a lot of preparatory work for the operation – first of all, I had to have the fitness tests on the bike once again. I didn't expect to do half as well this time, considering all the chemo I'd had, but Dr Carmen, the consultant anaesthetist, was very happy with the result, assuring me that I was still very fit and had strong lungs. I was quite chuffed with myself to be honest! I had loads of blood tests and so on, and everything seemed OK, so it was arranged for me to see Mr Skaiff for another colonoscopy. I wasn't looking forward to that, obviously, but he explained that I had to have it – the treatment to shrink the tumour on the bowel had been so successful that it wasn't easy to see it on the CT and MRI scans I'd had.

Before the colonoscopy I had to have an enema, another unpleasant but necessary procedure to clear the bowel so that the doctor could see it clearly. Anyway, the test was carried out, and Mr Skaiff put tattoo-like marks in the bowel to mark exactly which part he needed to cut out.

After a drink of water I was released from the unit and went to meet Becky, who was waiting for me in the car. I reached the car park barrier, saw Becky … and suddenly had the awful feeling of needing to evacuate my bowels – urgently! I did a quick u-turn and walked as quickly as I could to the nearest toilet. That was some enema.

Mr Malik arranged a scan for August to measure any growth in the liver, and I was given a date to attend Aintree Hospital for the operation on September the 1st 2015.

❧❧

Music has extraordinary power – to lift spirits, soothe a bruised heart, rouse a crowd or quiet an audience. Music is a very personal thing and sometimes, a perfect marriage of music, voices and lyrics can move someone like nothing else can.

I had the honour of working with Irfon for a very short time when I was a music therapist for Anglesey Council several years ago. I'll never forget the first time I met him at a mental health training session; 'Wow!' I thought, 'Who's this?' I could have listened to him all day – wise, intelligent, charismatic (and I might as well say it, good looking too!).

Hearing about Irfon's illness was a great shock, and when the Hawl i Fyw campaign was in its infancy I was invited, amongst many others, to join a Facebook group to discuss organising a concert in aid of the campaign. I remember feeling that a concert wasn't enough, somehow – we needed to spread the message across Wales and beyond and capture the media's attention in every way possible. Out of nowhere, two songs popped into my head: 'Perfect Day' and the Welsh Band Aid-style 'Dwylo Dros y Môr'. I Then thought of the classic Dafydd Iwan song of the same name as the campaign, and an idea was born. Recording a song like this would have a much larger impact than one concert. After talking to Irfon and Becky about it, it only took seconds for everyone to agree to go for it!

Well, where did we start? Fortunately, Elin Fflur was also a part of the team, and the two of us started organising things. The first stop was Sain Records and Dafydd Iwan, and in a meeting at the label headquarters in Llandwrog we, along with Irfon and his friends and the two Dafydds who run Sain, met to discuss the idea. As the campaign was a political one, we had to be sure that everyone was on board and were aware of the context. Irfon, as modest as ever, stressed that the message was not a personal one, but one which would benefit people the length and breadth of Wales, and Dafydd Iwan and Sain signed up without hesitation.

Elin and I compiled a long list of singers to sing a line of the song each, but would they agree to sing? And on a voluntary basis on top of that? I have no words to describe the unbelievable response to the invitation, and a few weeks later the Sain studio was crammed full of all the biggest names in the Welsh music scene, all singing their hearts out. Even Dafydd Iwan himself sung a line! Whilst I was conducting, I couldn't help but stare in awe at the sea of famous faces in front of me – it was like a dream!

Yes, it would be nice if it were all a dream and that there's no need to fight for Irfon's cause and the cause of many others in the same boat. In reality, Irfon was convalescing whilst we were in the recording studio, and although we all felt the excitement of singing and laughing together, he wasn't far from the thoughts of everyone taking part, especially Irfon's father who was singing with us as a member of the Brythoniaid Male Voice Choir.

We made the dream come true, and the media's attention was firmly on the song and the campaign for days afterwards; the CD sold out in the shops and topped the iTunes chart for weeks. Even now, it's included on Radio Cymru's Top 40 of the nation's favourite songs. Isn't that fantastic?

My heartfelt thanks goes to Elin for her hard work and to everyone who was part of the project, but the biggest thanks of all goes to Irfon for being such an inspiration to all of us.

Mari Pritchard

I'd followed Irfon and Becky's story, and met them to discuss their distressing situation. I saw in their situation a cruel example of the postcode lottery. A treatment existed that would be of benefit to Irfon. but for reasons that were nothing to do with him, that treatment was not available to him. On the other hand, it was readily available to those living 60 miles to the east of his home.

Irfon and Becky described and explained this injustice extremely effectively. The missing link was an official response, which would benefit not only Irfon but others facing the same situation.

The first obvious step for me was to raise the matter with the Prime Minister in Westminster. There came a chance when I was promised a question in his weekly Prime Minister's Question Time. This session is often raucous, with members shouting over each other noisily. But from time to time, an MP will raise a real issue, and the Prime Minister sometimes gives a sensible answer. This was what I hoped to achieve.

David Cameron's answer was sympathetic. But with a General Election on the horizon he questioned the Welsh Labour government's record on health issues. Cardiff answered back by disparaging England's Cancer Drugs Fund and boasting that their Welsh way was better, but finished by saying, 'we have no plans to introduce a cancer drugs fund in Wales.' Later on, however, the Welsh Government decided to revisit their policy, inviting Irfon to take part in the official review.

I hope that my input helped to persuade them to do that. But above all else, Irfon and Becky's amazing success in turning a personal tragedy into an inspiration for so many is an amazing and heart-warming feat.

Hywel Williams MP

Chapter 8

Aintree

On 23 July 2015, we were at last accorded the privilege of meeting Carwyn Jones, First Minister of Wales, at the Government offices in Llandudno Junction. Becky and I were very glad that he'd finally agreed to have an open discussion with us. He explained at the outset that he wouldn't make any comments or promise anything during the meeting, and that his main intention was to listen to our story, and to ask us for our opinion and recommendations with regard to changes to the access policy for uncommon or new drugs and treatments in Wales – focusing, of course, on Cetuximab, which had now worked in my case. There was only him, Becky and myself in the room, and he listened carefully to us for over an hour, questioning us about the process we'd been through. In fairness to him, I felt that he took us seriously, and that he respected the way we'd gone about things with regard to Hawl i Fyw/Fighting Chance. We told him of the English specialists' opinion about the efficacy of Cetuximab for some bowel cancer patients, and how the system in Wales didn't allow genetic tests to be carried out to strengthen the evidence of individual cases for IPFR. We made our comments very forthrightly about the IPFR process, the unfairness we'd felt as a family, the fact that inconsistencies were evident throughout Wales, and that we felt worthless throughout the whole process. At the end of the meeting, Mr Jones promised that he'd report back to his team on the evidence we'd submitted to him and would respond to us within two months with some kind of feedback. Becky and I felt that the meeting had gone well, and that we'd presented our comments unambiguously. We were confident that the issue would now at least be discussed.

The press had found out that the meeting had been held, and once again I was invited to speak live on the *Newyddion 9* TV evening news programme as well as on Radio Cymru the following morning. Newspaper journalists came to the house to interview me, and everyone expressed an interest in the content of the meeting and our opinion about it. I didn't want to go into too much detail about what had been discussed, but it was important for us to say that Carwyn Jones had given of his time to listen to us, and that we were confident of getting a concrete outcome to the meeting.

In August, Becky, Beca, Siôn, Ianto and I went to Spain on holiday. It was very hot there, and I had to be careful as I still had the rash from the Cetuximab. I really embarrassed Beca, bless her, by wearing, in her opinion, hats that were not cool!

Beca, Ianto, me and Siôn in Spain

Relaxing on holiday in Spain after my treatment

It was lovely to spend time relaxing, swimming, eating out and so on, simple things that were so important after such a hectic period. I also needed a break to prepare for what lay ahead of me in September. Looking back at the holiday, I was still a strong man, able to throw the boys around in the pool, swim and so on, and little did I realise at the time that I'd never be in such good physical condition again, after the surgery that I was facing.

To complicate matters further, we were going to move house after the holiday – a bit of an absurd thing to do, in retrospect. Life in Maes Berea in Bangor had been happy but the house was a touch on the small side, without much of a garden for the boys to play in. We saw a house and fell in love with it up in Bryn Adda in Penrhosgarnedd, a stone's throw from the hospital, and managed to buy it. The key transferral date was 3 September, when I'd be in hospital. I've occasionally been accused of being lazy, but going in to have part of my bowel and liver removed in order to avoid carrying heavy boxes was something everyone teased me about!

Nothing could have prepared me fully for the surgery. For some reason, I didn't feel much fear or anxiety this time. The previous year's liver op had gone so well and without a hitch, I thought that this one couldn't be much worse, and that I was strong enough to come through it and recover once again. This was my chance to beat cancer once and for all. I'd been through so much – the treatments, pain and stress – in order to get this opportunity. Becky and I stayed at a hotel in Liverpool the night before the operation and I was nicely relaxed and ready for it. Saying goodbye to the children hadn't been too difficult as I was so confident that everything would go well.

On the morning of 1 September 2015, I was in the theatre waiting room at Aintree Hospital by 7.30 a.m., and had said my goodbyes to Becky, who was intending to go shopping in Liverpool with a friend. Off I went to get myself prepared for surgery. The first person I met was a specialist colostomy nurse called Leanne. That was a bit unexpected to be honest, and as she explained that she was there to discuss the possibility that I might have a colostomy, I realised that was obviously on the cards, although Mr Skaiff had explained that there was also a possibility that I wouldn't need one. I accepted what Leanne had to say as she drew a circle in biro to the left of my belly button to show where the colostomy would be, if it were required. That's what was on my mind for the half-hour before going into the theatre – and unfortunately, bearing in

I loved it when the boys came to visit me

mind the experience I'd had a month earlier, I had to have another enema. Nasty old things.

I walked from the waiting room in my pretty nightie, a paper hat and stockings up to my hips in case I developed blood clots, through to the theatre to lie down on the bed. It felt good to hear Mr Malik's familiar voice and Scottish accent, and he spoke to me for a while to help me relax. He introduced me to the team and in no time at all, with a little medication and a mask over my face, I was out of it under the anaesthetic.

It was 9 p.m. when I came out of the theatre. Waking up after surgery, feeling confused and trying to make sense of everything, including people shouting my name to try and wake me up, is a strange experience. It was good to see Becky, who told me that, according to Mr Malik, the operation had been successful, and the tumours had all been removed. The next thing I remember is being lifted into a bed, and a crowd of people – doctors and nurses, I suppose – milling around me doing all kinds of things as I slipped in and out of consciousness. The only thing I can remember asking over and over again is 'Have I got a colostomy?' and they had to confirm the fact several times before I could make sense of the words.

My memory of the following days is a bit hazy, but I'd grasped that I was in intensive care, and I remember one particular nurse called Harry, who was older than the others and who took very thorough care of me. I remember whispering to him, for some reason, that he was an exceptionally good nurse, and thanking him for the little things he did to keep me comfortable.

Within 24 hours, I was able to start making sense of things. I remember, of course, that Becky was there at my side and that Mam and Clive also spent quite some time in the unit with me. A morphine pump was available to me, and it was important for me to press the button on it regularly when I felt pain, in order to keep myself comfortable.

On the second night, things deteriorated. I was vomiting a dark green bile, and one nurse tried his best to insert a nasogastric tube into my nose and down into my stomach to try to stop the vomiting. It transpired that my heartbeat was dangerously high, and the doctors were concerned about my blood pressure. I remember being rushed down a long corridor with Harry, a few porters and a doctor for a scan to pinpoint the exact problem. I remember asking Harry, 'Am I going to have a cardiac arrest?'. 'Not if I can help it!' was his reply. By the time I reached the scanning room, there was obviously great alarm about my condition because countless doctors had been called there to see me. Because of my medical background, I was in a better position than most to know that things didn't look good. I had a mask on my face, needles were being inserted into my arms and all kinds of medications were being pumped into me. I learnt later that I had an infection, and in the end they had to manage the situation with a cocktail of specialised medicines before taking me back to intensive care. I remember hearing one of the nurses talk about calling Becky, who'd returned to Bangor by then in order to take the boys to school on the first day of term. We were supposed to be moving house that day too, of course! When she got the call, Becky rushed straight back to Liverpool leaving her mother and other family members to move house for us.

Thankfully, things settled down after that nasty experience, and I had to come to terms with what had happened to my body. A tube led into my throat carrying medication and special fluids as well as antibiotics. I had a urine catheter and a pretty big scar on my stomach (obviously), and a colostomy, although I hadn't had a bowel movement at all for two or three days. The nurses explained to me that my intestine had entered something known as paralytic ileus, that is, the intestine was on strike and refusing to work, which meant that nothing passed from the stomach to the intestine at all. That explained why the tube in my nose was collecting the bile from the stomach. But the tube in my nose was nothing compared to the tube up my backside. That was painful, unpleasant and a nuisance to say the least. According to Mr Skaiff, I'd have to get used to it for the time being because it was set to be there for another week, at least.

I remember one terrible night in intensive care. I'd settled down comfortably and painlessly for the night, had been washed by Harry and was looking forward to a good night's sleep. A woman in a critical condition was brought to the bed next to mine, obviously in serious pain. It was impossible not to hear what was going on – she'd been in a motorbike accident and had broken more than thirty bones, if I remember rightly. She was screaming in pain and it didn't look as if I was going to get much rest.

Sleep was a very difficult thing to get on the unit anyway. I could hardly tell the difference between day and night at times and I started to steal a few minutes' nap whenever I could. I found it difficult not to focus on the clock on the wall opposite my bed, the tick-tock seemingly getting louder and slower during the night. For the first time I started to worry about my psychological state – the lack of sleep was having a negative effect on me, and I felt frustrated, a little scared and in low spirits. I remember thinking that I could see shapes of faces in the curtains, and talking to myself to try to make sense of everything. This was a combination of total exhaustion and the side-effects of the morphine, and after discussing the situation with the doctors I was given a drug to help me sleep at night, which was a tremendous relief.

As the week went on, I was obviously getting stronger. Becky visited me regularly, as did Mam and Clive, and Dylan and Glenna, Becky's parents, came to see me too. I was getting a little bit better every day, and could wash myself and sit up for a short while – the worst thing for me at this time was that

I couldn't drink or eat because of my intestinal predicament. I was terribly thirsty, and I felt so happy when one of the nurses suggested that I could suck an ice lolly. I remember being thrilled too when I was allowed to walk for the first time on 6 September, which is when the staff started to discuss moving me from the intensive care unit. After a whole week in the unit, I was moved to Ward 4 the following day.

I was familiar with Ward 4, of course, as I'd spent a few days there the previous year when I had the first operation on the liver. And although he didn't remember me at first, Mark, the one who was so nice to me at that time, was the nurse who welcomed me back to Ward 4. His humour was a tonic, and he spent a great deal of time with me explaining everything and assuring me that he'd do his best to keep me comfortable.

On Ward 4 there's no hope of taking things easy, and the physiotherapists were there first thing in the morning, ready to walk me up and down the corridor. I did this several times a day and was glad to be able to do it – although the tubes that were still attached to me were a bit of a nuisance. I got rid of the catheter after a while, and when Mr Skaiff removed the drain from my backside I was over the moon. Having the tube removed from my nose was a wonderful feeling too, and a sign that I was slowly getting better. The doctors started to discuss sending me home as they were very happy with the way I was

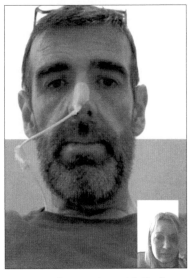

A Facetime session with Becky when I felt very low

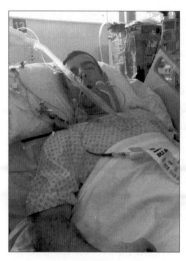

I was very unwell

getting over the experience. Of course, Mr Malik still came to see me regularly but I'd also taken a liking to two of his team, Mr Ed Alabraba and Mr Declan Dunn. They were both keen to see me get better, and were really nice people.

One morning, after being in Ward 4 for a week, I woke up feeling quite ill. Mark came to me and took my temperature, which was very high, indicating that something was wrong. I had to have an emergency scan that day, and it was late afternoon by the time I reached the Interventional Radiology unit. A scan earlier that day had shown an abscess in the liver which had obviously started to turn bad. I lay down on a bed over a scanner while a nice man named Dr Kumar treated me. He inserted needles in my side to kill the pain before inserting a needle and tube between my ribs and through to the liver. The pain was incredible but I felt a massive relief as over a litre of yellow-green fluid flowed out into a drain at the bottom of the tube. I was left lying on the trolley to regain consciousness.

Within seconds, I started feeling really ill, and unable to breathe properly. Dr Kumar and one of the nurses came over – once again my pulse was dangerously high. Within minutes, more doctors ran into the unit and started treating me by putting a mask on my face and needles in my arms. It turns out that this was the crash team, ready to start resuscitating me if it became necessary. The infection had got into my blood, and they were afraid I was suffering from sepsis. Although the doctors were keen for me to go back to intensive care, there were no beds available, so after I'd settled down about thirty minutes later, I returned to Ward 4, but to a private room this time, and a specialist nurse stayed with me for the rest of the night. By then, I'd realised that I had been on the brink of death.

Loads of my friends came to Aintree to see me after that, and it was nice to see familiar faces – and a few unfamiliar ones too! As I'd been in the public eye, people in Liverpool had heard about me and the campaign and had decided to come and visit me. One of those was Ann Gilpin, a nurse working in Aintree but who was originally from Cricieth. Her mother had been following my story in the press and on Facebook and persuaded Ann to come looking for me. Another nurse working in Liverpool came to see me too, a girl named Julie, whose family I knew from the Caernarfon area. Robyn Williams from Holyhead, a family friend and the family solicitor, had mentioned to me that his brother John lived in Liverpool, and that he was ready to help in any way. John came visiting regularly and we're now friends. I looked forward to visits by John Scouse, as he's fondly known, who always brought me a piece of home-made bara brith or something similar. John was a Medical Consultant working in the Runcorn area before he retired. He knew many of the doctors at Aintree, and was obviously a popular figure. He is also chairman of the Liverpool Welsh Society, and he sometimes used to bring me a copy of *Yr Angor*, the Society's magazine. It's a small world, and it turns out that John knew one of my old school friends, Gareth Endaf. Gareth and his two brothers, Arwel and Geraint, had trained as doctors in Liverpool and knew John well through the Society and the Welsh chapel.

As Aintree is the specialist hospital for liver treatments for north Wales it wasn't uncommon to meet other patients from Wales. Once there was a man from Holywell in the bed opposite me, and his family left him a copy of the *Daily Post* after one visit. I remember him looking at me in astonishment after looking at the paper, and announcing that there was an article about me in it, together with the announcement that I'd been nominated for an award. Bangor University, in conjunction with the paper, were setting up 'Leader of the Year' awards in north Wales. There were various categories, and I'd been nominated in the voluntary category because of my charity work and the campaigning. Very well-known names had been nominated, from the fields of sports, politics, business and public service. There were at least fifty names, and one award. Although I didn't know it at the time, I'd been invited to attend a ceremony at Bangor University that October, but I didn't think any more about it. My main focus, of course, was to get better.

I started to get to know the nurses very well, and I felt very safe in their care. Mark spent at least half an hour of his precious time talking to me every day, and another experienced nurse named Tina was great at explaining exactly what was going on in my body, how the treatment was working, and so on.

Unfortunately, the strong antibiotics I needed to treat the original infection in the intestine made me very ill, and I was vomiting frequently. One afternoon, I started to throw up into the washbasin by my bed, and felt an awful pain in my belly. I looked down and saw that my T-shirt was covered in blood. I called for the nurses by pulling the emergency cord and Mark and Tina rushed to my side. The scar on my stomach had burst, something that was known as wound dehiscence. After they took off my shirt I was able to see inside my own stomach – the muscles and the intestines – which left me in a bit of a state as you might imagine. Tina explained, while she tended to me, that one reason for this was that chemotherapy affected the body's ability to heal and scar. Immediately, Ed and Mr Malik were on the ward, and arrangements were made to take me back to theatre urgently to be stitched up. I had to receive two bags of blood after returning to the ward as I'd lost so much. The incident had a significant impact on me – I started to fear that something similar would happen to me again.

The next morning everything appeared to be fine, and Mr Malik was confident that the scar wouldn't reopen. The problem was, of course, that the new scar was very close to the colostomy and that great care would have to be taken when changing colostomy bags. Leanne, the specialist colostomy nurse, helped me to familiarise myself with the colostomy in no time. There was no pattern at all to my bowel movements, and I had to learn when to change bags and so on.

I wasn't at all upset about having to have the colostomy as it was a loop colostomy, that is, a temporary one – it could be reversed and the bowel could be stitched back together. One of the drawbacks of this kind of colostomy was that mucus could pass out of my backside, and for a while I couldn't feel when this was happening. It wasn't a nice experience to have to call the nurses to help me and to change my bed.

I was shortly back on my feet and walking up and down the ward in an attempt to get better so that I could go home as soon as possible. After the treatment my feet and legs had swollen enormously and were full of fluid – and the best way to get rid of that was to walk and move around as much as possible. Of course, that was quite painful at times, and as I tended to stoop as I walked Tina would come up behind me, give me a slap on my backside and pull my shoulders back, barking in her Liverpool accent, 'Straighten up, lad!'. Of course, I was instinctively protecting my stomach, as I was worried that the scar would open once again. I still had the drain from the liver in, as bile was still leaking from it following the surgery, and the drain from the bowel too, and I knew that those wouldn't come out until after I'd been sent home. As my scar was partly open in order to release fluid from it, I had a hole in the middle of my belly that was approximately the size of a 50p piece, and the intention was that it would scar from the inside outwards.

I started worrying about my mental health at that point. At times I felt lonely in the room on my own, and I asked to be moved to be with other patients in order to have some company, and make the most of the Scousers' wit! As I wasn't sleeping either, and was sick and tired of hospital food, I yearned to go home to Becky and the boys. One comfort was that the Rugby World Cup had started, and the matches held my interest daily. Messages from friends and family were a great help too, and the regular phone calls from Alan Owen and Gary took my mind off my condition. At times I needed a kick in the backside too, and I could depend on Robin McBryde for that. One day I must have (contrary to my usual nature) responded in a rather negative way to a text message from him, and I got this reply: 'Get a grip, don't moan, dig your heels in and get better so that you can come home, for God's sake'. That was exactly what I needed at times, and only close friends can say things like that with confidence.

On 22 September 2015, after almost four weeks in Aintree hospital, I was allowed home. The previous day Mr Malik had announced that my blood's CEA level (a measure of cancer activity) was down to four – excellent news which meant that there was no sign of cancer in my body. Saying goodbye to the nurses that day was an emotional experience, as I was fully aware of all they'd done for me over the preceding weeks. Mam and Clive came to fetch me, and I had quite a comfortable journey. Returning to a new house was a strange experience – this was the first time I'd seen our new home with the furniture and all our things in place. I immediately felt at home – and tearful – and seeing Becky waiting for me was a wonderful feeling. Dylan had bought me a special bed, fair play to him, similar to those in hospital but much more comfortable. (Hospital beds aren't made for people over six foot tall, in my opinion!) I tried sleeping in our bed with Becky that night, but in all honesty that was a mistake as I was tossing and turning, constantly getting up to go to the loo and getting up to change the colostomy bag. Lying down flat was painful and made me feel as if the scar was pulling, and lying on my right side was impossible because I still had the two drains. I kept Becky awake for most of that night, and we decided that I'd be better off sleeping in the spare bed until I'd settled down and established a regular sleeping pattern.

The next morning as I was lying in bed, it was a real pleasure to hear the boys run upstairs, full of excitement and very happy that Dad was home. Becky came into the bedroom after them carrying a cup of tea – the best I've ever tasted, I'm sure, out of a cup that wasn't made of plastic! The date was 24 September, the date of the award ceremony for North Wales Leader of the Year 2015 at Bangor University. Obviously, I was too poorly to go, so Mam and Clive went to represent me.

Becky and I were sitting in the living room when a Twitter message came through from Gareth Wyn Jones, the well-known local Tweeting farmer, congratulating me on winning the main prize! Very shortly Mam and Clive returned, full of pride, and confirmed that I'd won two awards in all. Poor Mam was a bit flustered as she'd had to deliver a short speech about me as she received the trophy.

I'd been described as

Mam receiving the award on my behalf

a hero and an inspiration to many because of my charity work and the campaigning, while I was going through cancer treatment myself. I really didn't feel like much of a hero sitting on the sofa, weak and thin, but I appreciated the award and accepted it not only on a personal level but on behalf of Becky and all the people who had supported me, especially the #HawliFyw #FightingChance committee.

The Hawl i Fyw / Fighting Chance committee

≈◊≈

I first met Irfon at my Hepatobiliary Clinic on 22/05/2014. Irfon was referred to me following chemotherapy for rectal cancer. At that time he was about to start radiotherapy.

At the point when I first met Irfon he had been through a lot in a short period of time. He explained that due to the restraints of treatment in Wales he had moved out of the family home and relocated to Manchester to receive necessary treatment for his rectal disease. Over the three years I have known Irfon he has been an advocate for service change in Wales. He has pursued this with vigour, even during the low times of his illness and in return he has helped a great number of Welsh patients along the way. From the first meeting I found Irfon to be a very inspirational man and I knew he would do anything in order to beat his disease.

Irfon is a great family man with five wonderful children and his wife Becky has been his most ardent strength throughout his illness. They have both remained strong and positive through the years and nothing has been too much trouble for them. Irfon also continued to highlight the need for change in treatment and has produced newspaper articles and has made a number of television appearances.

Unfortunately in 2017 Irfon developed disease progression with the added burden of lung metastases and he took this news with grace and dignity. I then referred him on to my colleagues for further treatment. Presently Irfon has advanced disease but through his determination and positivity he remains remarkably well with a good quality of life.

I can only say that Irfon has been inspirational. His strength and compassion for other patients through the roller-coaster of his illness has made him unique and I know that this resilience and positivity will be something that we will all remember.

Mr Malik

Chapter 9

Remission

Adapting to the new house was easy as it felt like home. There was far more space for the boys, and Becky was very happy with the kitchen as she loves cooking. She tried very hard to feed me up, but I was still having difficulty eating. This developed into more of a problem as time went on, and I had to focus on eating small snacks often. Whole meals were almost impossible, and I found it hard to settle into any kind of routine. As looking after me, not to mention Siôn and Ianto, was a full-time job, Becky had taken a spell off work, and was doing her utmost to prepare nutritious meals for me.

As I was so weak, we had to be careful that I didn't have too many visitors in the first few weeks. I hadn't actually realised how seriously ill I was. Manon Ogwen visited with a special cushion for me to sit on – I'd lost so much flesh from my backside that sitting down was painful. I spent most of my time in the living room watching TV, reading a little and listening to music. Unfortunately, I discovered television box sets and started watching *Game of Thrones*, and soon I was binge-watching programme after programme and really enjoying them.

When the boys came home from school I loved seeing them, but looking back I realise that I was pretty irritable, tiring quickly when I tried to play with them and often disappearing upstairs to lie down. I remember feeling guilty when Becky drew my attention to this. The two little ones understood that Dad was ill and needed a rest to get better, but naturally they'd also been missing me terribly, and were very eager for my attention. I tried to compensate for the situation by reading them bedtime stories, and singing them a little song before they went to sleep, as was our tradition at home.

I was still sleeping in the spare room as I was getting up several times during the night. Often the scar on my belly would seep blood and fluid, making a mess – in the early weeks I had two holes in it, a small one and a bigger one about the size of a 10p coin, and received a daily visit from the community nurses, usually in the mornings, to clean them. I'd been introduced to a couple of them after the first operation in August 2014, but I was going to get to know the team very well indeed now as it would take a long time for the scars to heal. The nurses' main role was to treat the scar but they also made sure that I wasn't developing any sores on the skin due to so much sitting and lying down. About two weeks after I arrived home I had an appointment at Aintree with Mr Malik and Claire to remove the drain leading to the bowel, which was quite a relief as it was painful. The liver drain came out too as Mr Malik was confident that the liver had healed and scarred.

A bedtime story

This made my life – and the community nurses' work – much easier.

One of the first community nurses I had dealings with was Bryn. I remembered Bryn working at Ysbyty Gwynedd years previously – he'd been my mentor when I was placed on the elderly day care unit. He was an extremely experienced nurse, a proud native of Caernarfon (a true Cofi as they're called) and quite a character. Also on the community team were Leah and Gill, and under their care the scars were healing well. Yes, it was a very slow process but by November the two holes had formed scars. I had a massive big scar down my belly and my belly button appeared to have travelled from its original position further to the right (it looked quite comical, in all honesty). As I started walking around a bit more and eating better the swelling in my legs went down, and suddenly I started putting on weight. I began to feel more normal, which was encouraging. It had been a difficult period for me but even more so for Becky, who'd been worried about my physical and mental health, and I wouldn't have been able to ask for better care from anyone.

Despite all this, I was still watching far too much television, and had now moved on to the *Prison Break* box set. I was still quite short-tempered with the boys, and with Becky too, I suppose. I remember Mam too saying that I was irritable and tetchy with her. This made me feel guilty, and I realised that I'd have to work hard to change the way I communicated with everybody.

Becky noticed that I was avoiding visits from friends and family, which was quite out of character for me. Lois called by fairly often and was anxious to know how things were going, and it was always good to see her and Beca. Owen, who was 16 at the time, didn't visit often at all, and was trying to avoid seeing me in my poorly condition as he found it difficult to cope with the situation. Although Lois and Beca had visited me in hospital Owen hadn't been able to. He'd discuss anything with me over the phone – football

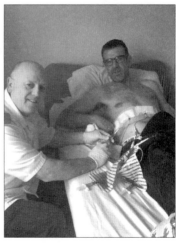

Bryn flushing the drain from the liver

usually – but he'd never talk about my health. Becky contacted some of our friends, and they gradually started calling again to see me. Alan, Gary and Aled Prys were regular visitors anyway, but the old rugby lads were very loyal too. Hugh Chink and Jon Kebab were in touch and called to see me from time to time, as well as Robbie and Richie, John Burns and Ian Roberts. I enjoyed their company, all of them, and realised that I'd missed this social contact.

Before long I'd gained enough strength to be able to go out for a walk and that kind of thing, and it was nice to be able to go and fetch Siôn and Ianto from school. I'd been avoiding that task for a while because I was fed up of repeating the same answers over and over as everyone asked me how I was, what the latest situation was, and so on. Obviously everyone was just being kind, while I was being touchy. Once they got used to seeing me on the yard people stopped interrogating me so much, and it was a relief just to talk about everyday topics with

Owen and me

the other parents and grandparents who were there to collect their children.

Hawl i Fyw / Fighting Chance was still going strong, and the committee had found out quite a bit about the process. People throughout Wales were sharing their stories and asking for advice on treatment access issues, and many were clearly finding it difficult to understand the IPFR system. Some didn't even know about it although they had cancer consultants looking after them.

The #teamirfon activities seemed to be slowing down, which was only natural when you consider how much money had been collected – over £100,000 by that time – but there were still many more fundraising activities in the pipeline.

Alan Owen and Stephen Edwards had arranged to do the 6 in 6 Challenge that October, namely to run the Snowdonia Marathon six times in six days, joining the official race on the last day. S4C's *Heno* programme was following their progress daily, and I needed to be in Llanberis on the first morning, 19 October, to support the lads. The TV crew was there and a lot of the villagers had come out to support them. I was given a great welcome at the Llygad yr Haul café on Llanberis High Street, who were supporting Al and Stephen that week. But the warmest welcome came from the pupils of Ysgol yr Hendre, Caernarfon, a brilliant gang who'd come there by bus with their teacher Eleri Ogwen, our friend Manon's sister.

During the week Robin McBryde came up from south Wales to lend his support, and in the company of Robin, his mother Diana and sister Naomi, I drove around looking for the two valiant runners who were supported by the faithful Gwyn Griffiths. Al had a tremendous shock when he saw Robin, and was obviously delighted that he'd come up to support him, but they didn't have much time to talk as they had to keep on running. On the Saturday, the day of the official race and the last day of the challenge, the Hawl i Fyw / Fighting Chance

The end of the 6 in 6 Challenge

committee were all there in support. I stood near the finish line to wait for them in the company of both their families, and when I saw Alan and Stephen run down Llanberis High Street carrying a banner bearing the slogan #HawliFyw #FightingChance it was impossible to fight away the tears. By the time Alan crossed the line I was a sobbing wreck. Without any doubt, the challenge and all the hard work had raised awareness in a big way for the campaign. The two runners had also raised a substantial sum of money for #teamirfon, and I'll be forever grateful to them both for what they achieved.

At the end of the Snowdonia Marathon that day, I started feeling unwell. Becky had suspected that something was wrong, and on the drive home I started shivering and feeling very hot. By the time we got home it was evident that my temperature was high – a sign of infection. We went directly to the Meddygon Menai unit, an out-of-hours GP service in Ysbyty Gwynedd, and I saw Janice Mercer's kind familiar face there. I was assessed and moved to Gogarth ward, and after asking the advice of Mr Malik's team at Aintree, the doctors there gave me an antibiotic. A few days later I was allowed home with a course of antibiotics, but within the week I was ill once more. Back I went to Ysbyty Gwynedd, but this time, again on the advice of Mr Malik's team at Aintree, an ambulance was booked to pick me up and take me off to Aintree. It was extremely busy there and I spent most of that night on a trolley in casualty as no beds were available until the next morning, when I was moved to an assessment unit. Becky joined me there the next day. I was immediately put on an intravenous course of antibiotics and a urine catheter was inserted. By the afternoon a bed had become free on Ward 4, and I got that safe feeling which I felt every time I landed there.

An urgent scan was arranged, and they found an abscess in the liver full of infected fluid. A rapid response was needed and in no time I was back in the Interventional Radiology department, ready to have a drain inserted into the liver once again. The doctor's name this time was Dr Davies, but I had the same nurse as before, Claire, who explained everything to me in detail. The entire treatment took about an hour and a half in all, and I didn't need full anaesthetic. The whole procedure was really painful, and when Dr Davies explained that he was going to insert the needle through the liver to gain access to the abscess I felt an acute pain. Even so, it felt good to feel the infection drain away, as if the pressure was released. The fluid filled the drainage bag and its colour looked quite noxious. No wonder I'd felt so ill. I had to stay on Ward 4 for another week to receive the specialist antibiotic, and because the condition of my veins was so bad I had to have another PICC line inserted in my arm. The nurses had to flush the drain with water daily to ensure that it didn't get blocked, which wasn't a pleasant sensation, and the community nurses would continue to do the same thing when I got home.

I had an appointment with Dr Mullamitha at The Christie on the same day as I was discharged from Aintree. Becky came to fetch me from Liverpool and off we went straight to Manchester. I was weak after the recent treatment but keen to discuss the next steps with Dr Mullamitha. He wasn't keen to give me any more chemotherapy, he explained, as my body had been through enough already, and needed to get better and stronger. He warned that it would take months until I felt well enough, but at the end of the meeting Dr Mullamitha said that he was very happy with everything, and announced officially that I was 'in remission'. There was no sign of any cancer in my body. I was crying as I left the room – I don't know why – but the tears were a mixture of elation and relief. I also felt guilt that I'd had an opportunity that wasn't available to other people, and glad at the same time that I'd managed to accomplish what I'd been fighting for.

Still, I found it hard to cope with the fact that I felt so weak and poorly. I hadn't felt so ill since the journey began, to be honest, and the latest operation had obviously knocked me for six.

After I got home, Dr Jones, my GP, made regular visits to monitor my progress. He tried to get me to understand that it would be at least six months before I was completely recovered. Nothing was too much for him, which made me feel confident to be able to ask for any advice or information. Very often in a situation like mine the patient's needs are given priority, but Dr Jones was keeping a close watch on Becky too, and was eager to support her. I know that that's been a tremendous help to her.

After the drain, Mr Malik had put me on a permanent course of antibiotics in order to attempt avoiding further infection in the liver. He was eager for me not to spend too much time in hospitals, and wanted us to be able to deal with the situation ourselves when I developed a temperature. This happened quite often, actually – I'd start shivering, feeling ill and getting hot. Becky came to recognise the early symptoms, and when that happened I'd go to the spare room, get undressed and lie on the bed in my underpants. That was a horrible feeling because a temperature makes you feel terribly cold. Becky would open the windows and sometimes turn the fan on, give me a paracetamol and put a wet flannel on my head. I'd have to stay there, freezing, until my temperature came down. This usually did the trick, and I'd very soon feel myself again.

As Christmas approached I was socialising more, and receiving regular invitations to speak publicly to groups and societies. I remember having to gear myself up many times before a public speaking engagement, and pushing myself to carry on, as I still felt weak and poorly at times. Becky used to send me to rest in bed for the afternoon when I was due to go out in the evening. But despite the tiredness it gave me great pleasure to speak about my story and journey. I received great feedback from Holyhead Rotary Club and a lot of laughs with the Menai Bridge WI. People were very kind and always eager to contribute towards #teamirfon by way of thanks, as I didn't charge a fee for my talks.

After discussing the matter with Becky, I realised that I was keen to do some kind of work. I didn't really want to work for the Health Board again, so I decided to set up my own little company, to give me something to do rather than to earn huge amounts of money. That was the beginning of Hanner Llawn Cyf. (translated as 'half full'), and the intention was to offer mental health training for companies, establishments and public services. The story soon got around, and gradually a little work started trickling in – enough to keep me busy for about a day a week, which was enough for me. Most of the work was in local schools, focusing on staff training, but unfortunately I had to postpone a number of workshops when I had infections. I remember feeling very ill during one presentation but I found strength from somewhere to finish the session before going home, shivering.

I hadn't published much on social media, and people were starting to ask how I was and what my health situation was. For some reason I was reluctant to announce that I was free of cancer and have a big celebration, but I decided that it was important for me to announce something in November 2015 as people were obviously interested in my case. I hoped that my story and attitude might help others, and judging by the goodwill messages and wishes I received, I think I succeeded in doing so.

Even so, I didn't always feel comfortable with the descriptions given to me. The word 'hero' was bandied about, but I really didn't feel like a hero. In his speech following the Leader of the Year award the Vice-Chancellor of Bangor University had described me as a 'reluctant hero', which was a better description, because I had a sense of responsibility for improving matters in Wales for the benefit of other patients, now and in the future. One young boy, Morgan Frazer (the son of Anest, one of my friends), had asked me for an interview for a school project. Morgan's a good lad, a real character, and of course I was willing to help. A short while later I received a message from Anest listing heroic people that Morgan had included in his project: I was at the top of the list, ahead of Nelson Mandela, Llywelyn the Great, Owain Glyndŵr, Mother Teresa and my friend, the opera singer Rhys Meirion! Now there's an honour, being higher than Rhys Meirion!

Following the announcement on Facebook, Hywel Trewyn of the *Daily Post* contacted me, and an article about me was published in the paper a few days later. I went on Radio Cymru too, talking on Dylan Jones's programme once again to share the good news that I'd beaten the cancer. It was a hard job to reply to the hundreds of messages of congratulations I received then. The problem was, of course, that I still felt very ill following the complications of the surgery, and it was very difficult to explain this to people who evidently expected me to be as fit as a fiddle.

As Christmas approached I received an email from Boom Cymru TV company, who were producing a programme for S4C called *Diolch O Galon* (Heartfelt Thanks) to be broadcast over the Christmas period. The purpose of the programme was to thank people all over Wales for charity work or some special achievement. But there was a twist in our story. Becky thought that the purpose of the programme would be to thank me for my charity work, but actually, it was to be an opportunity for me to thank Becky for everything she'd done for me. The researcher, Rachel Solomon (from Welsh pop group Eden and *Cyw* children's programmes) wanted me to think of someone famous who Becky admired or fancied! I drew up a short list – Mike Phillips, the rugby player, wasn't available but the popular singer Bryn Fôn was happy to be involved. An interview was

Filming the programme Diolch o Galon

arranged at our house presented by Rhys Meirion, before we went up to Ysbyty Gwynedd's Alaw Ward to record the rest of the item for the programme. Arrangements were made for Lois, Owen and Beca to arrive there with Bryn, so that we could turn the tables and focus the spotlight on Becky. Through my tears, I thanked her for everything before Bryn and the children came in, and was shocked when it was announced that there was a family treat arranged as a prize for us – a trip to Disneyland Paris. That caused quite a commotion, especially from Siôn and Ianto, and their excitement was plain for all to see in the programme which was broadcast on Christmas Eve.

In the weeks leading up to Christmas I was still suffering with the infections. Mr Malik had asked for a scan, and the results showed that the scars that had developed where the tumours had been cut out were preventing the bile from leaving the liver. As a result I was suffering from jaundice. The whites of my eyes and my skin were yellow and I was itching all over – one of the main symptoms. If bile doesn't leave the liver it can turn toxic and make you feel very ill. That explained why I'd been feeling so poorly. It was arranged for me to go to Aintree to have a stent inserted in the liver to try and open the blockage area and make space for the bile to travel to the intestine. I was on Ward 4 once again, but I wouldn't be there long – the treatment I needed was called ERCP (Endoscopic Retrograde Cholangio-Pancreatography), and administered in the endoscopy department. A nurse from that department came to explain the procedure to me – I'd be required to swallow a long plastic tube that would pass down through the stomach to the bowel, and up to the liver from there. The idea was that the tube would create enough space for the bile to bypass the scar, solving the problem. I would be administered a drug to make me relax, but I'd have to be awake for the treatment.

The doctors and nurses in the endoscopy unit were

cheerful and down-to-earth, and after having an injection in the back of my hand to deliver the medication to make me drowsy, I lay on my side. I started choking as the tube went down, but the experience was much easier than expected. I was discharged to go home the following morning.

About a week later I was sitting at the breakfast table with Becky when I felt a very odd sensation in the colostomy bag. There was obviously something wrong. Fair play to her, Becky cut the bag with a scissors. Inside it was what appeared to be a plastic spring, measuring about an inch long. Becky searched the internet and discovered that the stent that was in the liver had, in all probability, travelled down from the liver through the intestine and out into the bag! We spoke to Claire at Aintree, and after discussing the matter with Mr Malik she explained that it wasn't a common occurrence but that we needn't worry. But of course, a replacement would need to be fitted. I was called to Aintree for that procedure during Christmas week. There were no beds available for me in Ward 4 so I was put in Ward 10, which was an interesting experience to say the least. The nurses there were very kind, and I very soon learnt that this was a ward for people who had liver problems due to alcohol abuse.

There were four of us sharing a room, and the old fellow opposite me was obviously very ill. Next to him was a young man, Craig, who was in his late thirties and homeless, and next to me was a man of about the same age as me, Nigel, who was receiving quite a painful treatment. I'd thought I was a funny colour because of the jaundice, but Craig and Nigel were bright yellow. Craig was a hell of a case, a typical scouser, and he was constantly on the go. He'd say the funniest things completely out of the blue, making me laugh. 'Look at us,' he said one morning while we were eating breakfast, 'we're like a ward full of Minions!'. He was really kind to the man who was in the bed opposite me, helping him get a drink, talking to him and so on.

Christmas 2016

He asked me if I'd started the treatment to curb the urge to drink, and after I'd explained that I wasn't in for an alcohol-related problem, he started apologising and shaking my hand, obviously embarrassed that he'd compared our two situations. While I was there, Craig was visited by his social worker who told him that she'd found a bed for him in a hostel over Christmas. He was delighted at that, especially when he learnt that there was a large screen TV there too! I felt very fortunate that day.

There was a lot of laughter in the endoscopy unit when I went back there for my second stent, and the doctor joked that he'd just put the old one back in to save money. Once again the treatment passed without a hitch.

The next morning was Christmas Eve, and some of the staff on Ward 10 had started getting into the festive spirit. One of the nurses was dressed as a Christmas cracker, so I said to Craig, 'I'd pull her – would you?' Chuckling, he replied in his Scouse accent, 'That's a cracker, that one!' Despite the fun and games, I was pleased to see Dylan, who'd come to take me home.

Christmas was a very happy occasion that year. For some reason I was much stronger mentally than I'd been for some time, and the fact that I was in remission was a massive relief. Of course, I was realistic and realised that there was a possibility that the cancer could return, but for now I was free of it.

Spending time with the family has always been important to me, and Mam also puts great emphasis on that every Christmas. We have a tradition of spending a family day at Mam and Clive's house between Christmas and New Year every year, and that's often more exciting than Christmas day itself. It's always great to spend the day with all the children: the older ones, Lois, Owen and Beca, Luke and Holly (Arwyn's children), and Ffion and Elen (my stepbrother Andy's children) as well as all the little ones, Siôn and Ianto, Gruff, Gwion and Osian (Steve, my stepbrother, and Tracey's children, who had all come over from Brussels) and Sophie and Zac (the children of Melanie, Luke and Holly's mother – yes, my family can be complicated!). Mam and Clive's close friends have the honour of attending the family day too, and a good time is guaranteed with Auntie Shwsmi, Mam's best friend, and Nerys and Dave.

Claire contacted me from Aintree after Christmas. The stent in the liver hadn't worked and that meant going back to the Interventional Radiology department for a PTC (Percutaneous Transhepatic Cholangiogram). The original drain from the abscess was still in and collecting bile, but another one had to be inserted to prevent the bile from accumulating in the liver. That was what was causing the infections and jaundice, and making me feel so ill. On 30 December I was back on Ward 4 at Aintree receiving the usual welcome from the nurses, and the treatment had been arranged for the next day, New Year's Eve.

Late that night I received quite an unexpected message from a member of staff at Radio Cymru at the BBC in Bangor. They'd received a confidential statement about an announcement due to be made the following day regarding the drug Cetuximab. Apparently, the All Wales Medicines Strategy Group were stating that there was evidence that the drug was effective in the case of some bowel cancer patients, and were recommending that the drug should be available in Wales as an early treatment for those patients. I was delighted, to say the least, and had a big smile on my face. Radio Cymru wanted me to speak on the *Post Cyntaf* news programme the next morning, and of course I was ready to participate. On hearing the excellent news I felt really proud of the work that #HawliFyw #FightingChance had accomplished – without a doubt, the campaign had influenced the decision. I was happy too that Carwyn Jones had kept his word. The following morning, I spoke on air from my bed in Aintree, saying that the move was a major step forward and was going to save lives in future, but that I was sad and angry that the decision hadn't been made much sooner, considering how many people would have benefited from it in the past. This was proof too that campaigning did have a purpose.

That afternoon, I was in the Interventional Radiology unit. Dr Kumar was going to attempt to insert another stent by some complicated process, and if that wasn't successful he was going to have to put another drain in the liver. Before I signed the consent form he explained that 30% of people die within a

*Although I was very weak, I made an effort to go down
to the rugby club to watch the boys train*

month of receiving the treatment, which came as a bit of a bombshell, but Dr Kumar assured me that he personally hadn't experienced that throughout his career. Although he'd allayed my fears to some extent I started thinking about all the children and felt a wave of sadness engulf me. The nurse and Dr Kumar realised how I felt, and were both very kind with me, giving me plenty of time to pull myself together before the treatment started. According to Dr Kumar, his mother had received the same treatment as me and she too had taken a long time to get better.

Unfortunately, despite trying more than once Dr Kumar couldn't get a stent or tube past the scar tissue. He was apologetic, and obviously disappointed at having to change the plan and insert another drain in the liver, about an inch away from the original drain. He decided that another one was needed too, in the middle of my chest and into the other side of the liver. So there were three drains in my chest attached to

Clive, Steven and I supporting the Scarlets

bags which held the bile, and I was going to have to tie them to my legs to walk around for quite some time.

Arrangements were made for the community nurses to call daily to flush the drains (a very painful process), and soon I was home. I have to say, although I was still weak and the drains were extremely uncomfortable, that I felt a bit better. Mr Malik was going to monitor me closely, but he warned that the drains would stay in for some time.

I was given the honour of wearing Welsh radio host Geraint Lloyd's famous travelling hat

✥

I met Irfon for the first time in September 2015 in Aintree Hospital, Liverpool. I felt it a duty, as a member of the Liverpool Welsh community, to meet and congratulate this special man I'd heard so much about in the media because of his Hawl i Fyw campaign. I took him a copy of our local Welsh paper, Yr Angor, and very soon we were chatting as if we'd known each other for years. I found him a friendly, welcoming and modest man, a true Welshman whose humour shone through even when he was tired and in great pain. In spite of his gratitude to his medical team, it was plain enough to see that he was itching to leave hospital and get back to Rebecca and their sons.

One of Irfon's most obvious traits is his positive outlook in every situation. It would be so easy for him to be bitter and angry about his predicament, but that wasn't Irfon's way.

This is the man who inspired #teamirfon to raise over £150,000 towards Ysbyty Gwynedd's Awyr Las appeal following his cancer diagnosis in 2014. He decided to work alongside the body which refused to fund his treatment, in order that others facing the same cancer battle should receive the same treatment as patients in the rest of the UK.

One of Wales' great poets, Waldo Williams, wrote a couplet which sums Irfon up:

Daw dydd y bydd mawr y rhai bychain,
Daw dydd ni bydd mwy y rhai mawr.
                              Waldo Williams

Loosely translated, it means that one day, ordinary people will triumph and the ones in power will fall from grace. Irfon is no longer one of the ordinary people – he's a giant of a man. I'm grateful I got to know him.

Dr. John Williams, Liverpool

Chapter 10

Fear Knocked on the Door

It was January 2016, nearly two years since the original diagnosis, and it had been a tempestuous two years to say the least. It was only when I stood back and considered everything I'd been through that I realised what a big challenge the whole thing had been. While undergoing the treatment I'd kept my head down and concentrated on that – there was no other option. What would have been the point of feeling sorry for myself?

But by now, I was feeling a bit lost, and finding it hard to cope with the situation of being free from cancer, and the fact that everyone seemed to be celebrating on my behalf, happy that I'd beaten the disease. I felt frustrated that I couldn't make people see that I was fragile – physically and mentally – and that I needed to look after myself.

My eating pattern was very poor. I couldn't sit at the table to eat without gagging, and I threw up often. Becky found that very hard to deal with, and it was a constant bone of contention between us. It was impossible to tell whether this was a physical or psychological problem – Becky believed that it was psychological, while I was convinced that it was a combination of both.

The community nurses were still visiting every day to treat the three drains and flush each of them out with water, which was painful and quite nasty at times because the bile sometimes leaked out. The dressings around the drains had to be changed daily and I had to just hope that they wouldn't leak again before the nurses returned the following day, but that did sometimes happen and I'd have to change the dressings myself. Carrying the three drainage bags around was a bit of a pain at times as two of them were tied to my right leg and the other to the left. I had to lay them out carefully at night, trying not to pull them or lie on them in my sleep. Unfortunately, a rancid smell emanated from them from time to time, and I went through a small fortune's worth of aftershave to try and mask it, although Becky insisted that it wasn't that bad. Nobody complained, anyway (apart from Becky!), but having said that, it was probably highly unlikely that anyone else would tell me that I stank of cabbage!

I longed to do the little everyday things that people take for granted. I couldn't have a nice shower because I had to keep the dressings dry, and I had to hold the drainage bags in one hand while washing myself with the other. Of course, Becky often gave me a hand, giving my back a good scrub! Swimming was another thing I couldn't do, and I'd always loved taking the boys down to the swimming pool.

Sian Morgan Lloyd from ITV contacted us again – she was the one who'd produced the *Byd ar Bedwar* and *Wales This Week* programmes about me the previous year. There was talk that S4C were interested in commissioning another documentary about me, a follow-up, in a way, but with a more personal angle this time, rather than political. Becky and I were happy for that to be done if the demand was there for another programme, and Sian promised that she'd keep in touch to discuss recording dates and so on.

Although I still wasn't eating properly the situation was improving thanks to Becky's perseverance. I could socialise fairly well, and family life was pretty normal apart from the infections I continued to pick up from time to time. I hoped the drains could come out one day, and Claire Burston, my nurse at Aintree, used to get in touch regularly for an update on my condition and to ask for an occasional blood test. In

Becky and I

Sian Morgan Lloyd and Rhys Edwards

Filming the documentary O'r Galon *for S4C in Rome*

February Mr Malik asked for a liver scan to assess the situation as regards the regular infections, and explained that he intended giving me further operations to treat the scar tissues that were causing the blockages as well as to get rid of the abscess.

On 2 March 2016 Becky and I were having lunch in the Ysbyty Gwynedd canteen following one of my appointments with the dietician when Becky's phone rang. It was Claire calling, and from her voice it was evident that she had bad news. Becky asked her bluntly if the scan showed any cancer, and Claire confirmed it without going into too much detail. She'd arranged for me to see Mr Malik in his clinic at Aintree the next day, she said, to discuss matters.

That night and the following morning's journey to Liverpool were difficult because we weren't quite sure what the prognosis would be. Still, our faith in Mr Malik was strong and I was certain, whatever the situation, that he'd have a plan. We received the usual welcome from Mr Malik and Claire before sitting down. What he had to say came as a bit of a shock. He explained that four new tumours had appeared on the liver, but that in addition to this the cancer had spread to both lungs as well. Mr Malik has always spoken honestly to us and I was aware that we were no longer talking about getting better or beating the cancer, and that the focus of the treatment now would be to keep me alive for as long as possible. If I'm being perfectly honest, I'd already accepted that. The cancer was obviously determined and obstinate and had reappeared in the liver three times by then.

Mr Malik explained that the lung tumours weren't big and weren't likely to cause any trouble. He'd discussed my case with a specialist at the Liverpool Heart and Chest Hospital in Broadgreen. His name was Mr Shackloth, and he was willing to accept my case and treat the lungs there. But before that, we had to set about dealing with the liver situation, because, in Mr

Malik's words, 'That's what will kill you, not the lungs'! His intention was to continue with the liver treatment plan, while also trying to get rid of the tumours. He was going to have to carry out quite an unconventional procedure that would involve stitching two sections of the intestine onto the sides of the liver and creating a pathway for the bile to pass from the liver to the intestine. The treatment would probably leave me with about one quarter of my liver remaining.

He explained that it would be my choice whether to accept the surgery or not, and that a course of chemotherapy would have to be considered. He warned that this could cause problems with infections, especially as the drains were still in, and that this, in the end, would be what would most probably kill me. Added to that, there was an enormous risk of heart failure or a stroke during the operation too, and a possibility of liver failure, especially in the first days after the treatment. I would spend about twelve hours in theatre, and Mr Malik had asked a colleague of his, Mr Fenwick, another prominent consultant surgeon from Aintree Hospital, to accompany him during the surgery.

Following the conversation with Mr Malik, Claire took us to another room to explain everything again in detail to make sure that we fully understood what the possibilities were. Becky asked what would happen if my liver failed – the answer was that I'd be none the wiser, as I'd be unconscious on a life support machine, and Becky would have to make the decision to switch it off, when the time came. In truth, Mr Malik had made it clear that the surgery was the only option in his opinion, despite the risk. There was no other choice in my opinion either – if I was going to die I much preferred to go down fighting, and to go for it with the surgery. A line from one of my favourite films, *Highlander*, came to my mind: 'It's better to burn out than to fade away' – and that's exactly how I felt at the time. Of course, for Becky, this meant the possibility that she would face losing me the following week. It would be a difficult week for her, and the day of the operation itself would be even harder.

We needed to talk to family and close friends about the situation. Steve, my stepbrother, had been in a meeting in Cardiff and had decided to travel to Mam and Clive's house in Talwrn for a few nights in order to spend some time with me, and we had a good talk. He'd been hit hard when Arwyn died, and had felt out of touch because he was living so far away in Brussels. Naturally, Mam was very emotional and wanted to spend as much time as possible with me that week. I only spoke over the phone with Dad – he had a heavy cold and didn't want me to catch it. I don't know how he'd have coped anyway. On the Monday evening, we had a meal in Llandudno and Becky and I spent a cheerful evening in the company of Lois, Beca, Siôn and Ianto. I had a chance to speak to the girls about the possibilities of the surgery. Owen wasn't available to come with us as he was working, and I'm not sure how he would have coped either. I found it hard myself, especially on saying goodbye to the girls with kisses and tearful hugs.

Becky had explained matters to my friends, and Alan and Gary came to see me. Robin sent me a text on the night before the operation which made me think, and which gave me a peculiar strength:

> Fear Knocked on the Door
> Faith Answered
> There was No-one there

I posted this on Facebook and the response was incredible. I slept well that night, and in the morning there was no time to overthink things. Mam and Clive came to pick up Siôn and Ianto, and I managed not to cry in front of them. The two little ones were always sad, especially Siôn, before I went to hospital, and I didn't want to upset them any more than usual. They went off in the car quite contentedly with Nain and Taid.

Becky and I took the opportunity to discuss matters during the journey to Aintree. She found it difficult to think of what was ahead of us but I'd found strength from somewhere, and was determined that I wasn't going to die during the surgery. I don't know why or how, but I was definitely going to come through it.

At Aintree, we saw Mr Malik and Mr Fenwick and some of the team, including Ed Alabraba, on their way to theatre. Knowing that these three were going to be

Sayng our goodbyes at the theatre door before the third operation on my liver

looking after me gave me faith – I had so much respect for them, and I felt that they respected me too. Ed had told me before that Mr Malik had a strong feeling of responsibility for me, and was ready to do anything in his power to keep me alive for as long as possible. He told Becky too, 'Mr Malik has an investment in Irfon'. The truth was that not many doctors in his shoes would have risked embarking on such a complex surgical process.

I was due to go to theatre at 11 a.m. As relatives weren't allowed in the theatre waiting room, one of the nurses gave us permission to sit outside until it was time for me to go in to get prepared. I remember Becky looking at me anxiously, wondering whether that would be the last time she saw me alive. But I remember saying that I wasn't going to die.

I was escorted down to a room outside the theatre, where

I saw the anaesthetist. I felt quite confident as I walked down to theatre and soon I had the anaesthetic in my arm and the mask on my face, and I closed my eyes.

Becky faced a very long day. She'd arranged for her friends, Sarah and Manon Ogwen, to come to Aintree to support her, and that made me feel calmer. To pass the time, the three went out for lunch and a bit of shopping before returning to the 'hotel', namely the hospital's accommodation for patients' relatives. They were outside the intensive care unit at about 9 p.m., hoping for some news. The nurses hadn't heard how I was, but the theatre had called for my bed – a sure sign that things were almost drawing to a close.

By midnight I was back in intensive care, with a ventilator breathing on my behalf. Various needles and tubes entered veins in my neck and arms, and I had drains in my nose and stomach, and a urine catheter. I wasn't aware of this at the time, of course, as the doctors had given me strong medication to keep me in a coma. In the meantime, and despite having just spent over twelve hours working on me in theatre, Mr Malik went to see Becky, Sarah and Manon. He spoke truthfully and bluntly to Becky – he'd done all he could, and the only thing he could do now was hope for the best. Really, he was warning her that there was a real chance that I was going to die, and that she had to brace herself for the worst as I was in a critical condition. By the time he finished speaking, even Mr Malik himself was tearful. Manon went over everything again with him, to make sure that Becky was processing the information. Manon phoned my family – Mam, Dad and Lois – to give them all the information, and suggested that they should travel up in the morning to be with me. Becky left a message for Gary, and he travelled to Liverpool the next morning too.

Becky and Manon came in to the unit to be with me. Sarah couldn't face seeing me in that condition, so she stayed in the family room. The nurse caring for me confirmed that I was really ill, and that the next few hours and days would be touch and go, as they were closely monitoring the condition of my liver. Becky held my hand and said, crying: 'I love you, Irfon, and if you could hear me now I know you'd say that you love me too.'

Without any warning I lifted my head up off the pillow and raised my arm into the air as if I was reaching out to her. I was obviously responding to Becky's words, but the nurses started to worry – I needed to be sleeping more heavily and for longer, so the level of sedation was increased.

Although Becky and the girls returned to the accommodation, they didn't get much sleep as I understand it, as they were phoning the unit nearly every hour to ask whether there was any change in my condition. I, on the other hand, apparently had a stable, comfortable night under the excellent care of the special nurses.

The next morning I was still on the vent, but as I'd been more stable overnight, the nurses were keen to get me off it and to put me on a lower dose of sedation. I felt completely different to the way I'd felt after all my previous operations – after all, the operation had been such a lengthy one – but I was conscious that they were reducing the dosage of drugs that kept me sedated as I could hear voices. They asked me to squeeze Becky's hand to show that I could hear them, and I managed to do that. I opened my eyes and started teasing them straight away, poking my tongue out at Manon and joking that Mam, who had by then arrived with Clive and Lois, was talking too much by making hand signals to imitate her mouth jabbering on.

Gary arrived at the unit. Despite not being able to talk, I looked at him, and he looked back at me, and we both understood each other perfectly – we were both appreciating the beauty of Sarah Louise, the Irish nurse who was looking after me! She, like all the other nurses there, was friendly,

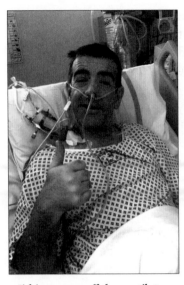
I'd just come off the ventilator

especially good at her job and very careful with me.

During the ensuing few hours, the doctors decided that I was well enough to be taken off the vent. Becky was thrilled – as was I, naturally. I announced to everyone that I loved life, and that I was right when I'd said that I was going to survive the surgery, contrary to all expectations.

Mr Malik came looking for me once more in the intensive care unit, and was all smiles as he approached, celebrating the fact that I'd got over the worst of it, although he did warn me that the condition of my liver would need to be very closely monitored for at least three days. I was recovering very quickly, and everyone was very happy about that, including my family and the medics. I spent the rest of the day resting, with Becky by my side.

The next morning, as was the tradition at Aintree Hospital and their Enhanced Care Programme, they were keen to get me up and out of bed quite sharpish to start moving about, and two physiotherapists approached me early in the morning after I'd finished eating my breakfast (my first in three days). I argued with them a little bit – I didn't feel too special – but physios, in my experience, tend to be quite determined people, and they managed to persuade me to get up. I walked to the side of the bed, but can remember nothing of what happened next. I fainted, and was out cold for nearly half an hour because my blood pressure was so low. I was rushed to the CT scan unit in order to assess if I'd sustained any damage when falling.

When I got back to intensive care, the consultant explained that both my lungs had collapsed. This meant a whole day of a treatment called CPAP, to help with my breathing, and I had to wear a strange-looking mask and helmet contraption. What it does is increase the air pressure in the throat, in order to enable the lungs to reinflate to their full size.

I got better very quickly after that, and as there was no television at all in the intensive care unit, I had to beg the consultant there and Mr Malik to be moved back to Ward 4 by the following day, Saturday 12 March, when Wales were playing England in the Six Nations' Championship. Fair play to them, they were both very supportive, although there was a bit of banter and leg-pulling between us: Mr Malik is a Scot, the other consultant was English, and I, of course, am Welsh! We lost that day ...

Being back on Ward 4, as always, made me feel safe, in the hands of the familiar nurses. This is when I met Ann properly – a nurse who is now one of my favourites as well as being a good friend. Obviously, the other nurses knew me well by now, and I'm sure the rest of the patients must have been wondering what on earth was going on when they saw them all come over to hug and kiss me when they started their shifts on the ward!

Over the next few days, I started to feel quite a severe pain in my stomach. One of the things that made me happiest after the surgery was getting rid of the three drains I'd been carrying around with me for three months, and I hoped that this pain wouldn't put that in the balance. But apparently I'd developed another infection. Bile was leaking from the liver creating an abscess in my stomach under the area of the colostomy. Unfortunately, the scar this time was bigger than the others and Mr Malik had explained to me that it was even more difficult to open up the flesh and muscles to get to the liver because all the previous operations had produced adhesions – scars and hard skin that had stuck together, and possibly to

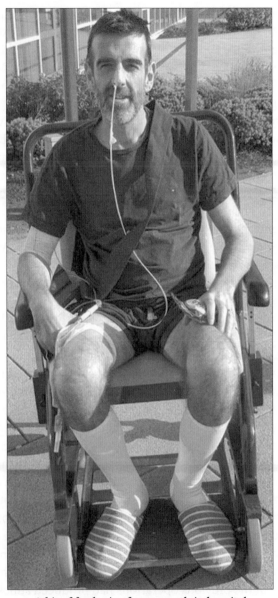

A bit of fresh air after a month in hospital

other organs. Ed Alabraba had to remove stitches from the top of the scar and leave it open, as bile was leaking from the liver to the scar tissues well (which by now measured the size of a 50 pence piece, directly under my ribs). The hole caused a mess frequently – at least once an hour and sometimes more often – emitting a mixture of bile and blood, and so I had to lie down flat on my back all the time. Ann decided that she would take responsibility for my care, and I can't think of anyone better equipped for the task. Nothing was too much trouble for her – she'd spend hours with me trying to ensure that the lesion didn't make a mess, but with very little success. Ann asked Leanne, the specialist colostomy nurse, for help, and Leanne tried using colostomy bags to catch the bile. They leaked, and nothing else seemed to work either. One of the nurses on the shift managed to stop the lesion overflowing for a little while longer than the others, but even that was only about two hours. As you can imagine, the situation impacted my sleep in a major way. In the end, despite all the efforts made, I had to accept the situation, and Ann committed herself totally to the job of cleaning the lesion regularly and keeping me clean and dry at all times. I appreciated that very much indeed.

Unfortunately, due to the abscess in my stomach, I had to go back once again to the Interventional Radiology department, where Claire, the nurse, and Dr Kumar were waiting for me. They were ready to insert another drain. I wasn't entirely happy about it, but I accepted that this, unfortunately, was the best thing to do. A drain was inserted into my liver – and it's a good thing that it was, because nearly two litres of fluid came out of it, which had obviously turned bad as its colour was a noxious yellow-green colour. If it hadn't been released, it would have been enough to kill me.

Back on the ward, everything went ahead as planned. I was put on a course of antibiotics, and as my veins were so weak after all the ill-treatment they'd suffered, I once again had to have a PICC line inserted in my arm, to enable the antibiotic to reach the body more easily. I understand now that the infection (as things have been for me since the beginning) was an unusual one, so I had to have quite specialised drugs to treat it.

One of the things that caused me concern was the fact that I couldn't eat properly. This has been a recurring problem throughout my treatment, but this time I was losing weight rapidly. The nurses were worried about me and offered to bring me food from outside the hospital, to let me go to the staff canteen and to order special foods from the hospital kitchen. We didn't have much success, to be honest, and I was still losing a substantial amount of weight. A dietician named Lisa came to see me, and she decided, after discussing the matter with Mr Malik and myself, that I would have to be given a nasogastric tube (that is, a tube from the nose to the stomach) in order to feed me overnight with over a litre of highly nutritional liquid.

Having the tube inserted down my nose was a horrific experience, and Vanessa, one of the nurses I was very fond of, had a hell of a job trying to keep me still in order to complete the job. She succeeded in the end, although I'd vomited all over the place! I received the liquid through the tube that night, but had to keep trying to eat as much as I could in order to get the necessary carbohydrates and calories. The problem was that I threw up when I tried to do that because the feeling of having the tube down the back of my throat was so uncomfortable, and as I vomited the tube came out with the food. That happened on two occasions.

In response to this, it was decided to introduce a different tube called a nasojejunal tube instead of the nasogastric. This tube's function was to take the liquid down further than the stomach, into the bowel, and I had to go down to the endoscopy unit to have it fitted. Although I'd felt quite apprehensive before going for the treatment, it passed quite smoothly. The only snag was that the tube came out of my nose and hung down to my knees, almost! According to Lisa, the dietician, this was a very stable tube – there was no chance of it coming out by accident if one of the boys (or I!) started messing with it.

As the antibiotics I was on were specialised, I needed a long course of them. Despite this, Mr Malik was keen for me to be allowed home from hospital and to receive the rest of the drugs through the PICC line in the community rather than on a hospital ward. When he was informed that that service wasn't available twenty-four hours a day from the community nurses in north Wales, he was very disappointed. Mr Malik started bargaining with the health board in Bangor to establish some kind of service for me, but until he succeeded, I would have to stay at Aintree.

Meanwhile, the incredible Manon Ogwen from Alaw Ward was on the case, and while she discussed the matter with the cancer services managers, it was decided to transfer me to Alaw Ward to receive the treatment there. No, I wasn't going to get to go home, but this was close enough. Being moved to Bangor would make life much easier for Becky, who was travelling every other day to Liverpool to visit me.

The journey from Aintree to Bangor went amazingly quickly, and when I arrived at Alaw Ward I felt a wave of happiness engulf me on seeing the familiar Welsh-speaking faces there to welcome me, with Becky, Siôn and Ianto amongst them. The boys were thrilled that I was coming home – or closer to home than before, at least!

One of the things I remember from being on Alaw Ward that time is Siôn saying 'Dad has shrunk' – which confirmed how much weight I'd lost, and the physical and mental effects of my treatment on me.

While I was on Alaw, the community nurses came in every day to receive training from the ward staff on how to treat PICC lines, and how to administer the necessary drug to me when I returned home. After a while, I was allowed home, but had to report to Ysbyty Gwynedd every morning to receive the antibiotic, a process which took about two hours, and then go home. I had to go back to the hospital at 8 p.m. to receive the day's second dose of the drug, and my friend Aled Prys was very good at coming to keep me company on Alaw during these periods. One evening, Aled brought his ipad in with him so that we could watch a Liverpool match together. What a brilliant idea, I thought, but I couldn't believe my eyes when he pulled something else out of his bag – a bottle of beer, to enhance the experience! Mind you, he only had one bottle, as I wasn't drinking …

With five days of the treatment left, the arrangements had all been made for me to receive the antibiotic at home. So from 12 April onwards, the community nurses would come to our house twice a day to treat the PICC line and administer the drug to me. Although this only lasted a few days, the community nurses' training didn't go to waste, and by now, this new service is offered all over the area, so that anyone who's in the same situation can come home from hospital earlier and receive treatment through a PICC line in their own homes. The thanks for that go to Mr Malik and Manon Ogwen.

It felt good to be back in my own bed again – and even better being able to share that bed with Becky without affecting her sleep too much! Another good feeling was having one drain coming out of my body rather than the three I'd been putting up with for six months.

By now, I weighed less than ever before. From being a big lad, weighing around 15½ stones all my life, I now weighed less than 10. I was conscious that I looked unwell, all skin and bones, and Becky tried to tease me by saying that I'd forgotten to bring my backside home with me from Liverpool! But it was no laughing matter – Becky had a bit of a shock when she saw how thin I'd become as she was helping me wash myself in the shower. My muscles had disappeared and the outlines of my bones were clearly visible under my skin. The experience I'd had a year or so earlier when my scar had opened as I threw up was still affecting me, and facing food was difficult. I had to start creating a new eating pattern, i.e., little and often. Proper meals were still not possible – I'd have vomited them back up straight away. It was very hard for Becky, poor thing, to deal with that situation yet again.

After discussing the issue with the teams at Liverpool and Bangor, they decided to refer me to a counsellor to see whether discussing the problem might help, but I didn't gain much benefit from that. In the meantime, even the nasojejunal tube had come out as I threw up – apparently, that was a very uncommon occurrence. I was then referred by the Aintree team to the local psychologist in Bangor, but as I knew the team there well, I saw a psychologist who worked in the Conwy and Denbigh area.

I didn't feel that anybody properly understood the predicament I was in. To tell you the truth, I started to get fed up with people suggesting things that might help me – things like eating ginger biscuits and drinking mint tea. Once again, I didn't get answers to the problem by seeing the psychologist.

Although I didn't agree with her, Becky was adamant that the situation was developing into a psychiatric problem. Having said that, I was willing to try anything that might help me eat better. It's true that I suffered mild depression during this period – and I think it's important to be strong enough to admit that too. Many people find it hard to discuss matters like this, especially men, for some reason.

When I went to see him about the matter, the doctor asked me some quite scary questions, like did I feel depressed enough to consider suicide. Apparently this is a routine part of all assessments, but I think he got the message from me in no uncertain terms – that would never be something that I would consider as an answer to any problem, and I intended to battle on until the very last breath. He gave me anti-depressant medication, which has helped somewhat to relieve my anxieties, and works hand in hand with the complementary therapies that I've been using, especially the sound therapy.

I never imagined that I'd use complementary therapies. Not that I've ever criticised that kind of thing, but since my first time on Alaw Ward I'd noticed how many people got pleasure from them, especially reflexology, which is a method of massaging the feet where every part of the foot is linked with some organ or body part. Reiki is offered too, but I didn't feel that I'd get as much out of that as from the reflexology and the relaxation sessions. I'd started practising mindfulness before I was diagnosed with cancer, and that was a great help too.

I was invited to give Sound Healing a go by a woman named Steph Healy (a good name for a therapist, I thought ...) and at the time I didn't have much idea what it was. I have to admit that I was a little bit cynical at the start, but when I got to Steph's house in Mynydd Llandygai for the first time, she explained that it wasn't a miracle therapy, and that everyone got different benefits from the sessions. I decided I'd give it a go, and after just one session I knew I'd carry on with it.

For the sessions, I'd lay down comfortably on the floor of a shed at the bottom of Steph's garden. Around me were four gongs, Tibetan bowls, bells and all kinds of other unusual instruments. The session started with what's known as a body scan, a technique to make you relax before starting on the sound. When I went for my first session I didn't have a colostomy, and the tumour in my bowel meant that I found it very difficult to go to the toilet. After that first session of a little over an hour I was totally relaxed and felt very at ease. I don't know how or why, but after I got home I had the best bowel movement that I'd had in months!

By now, mindfulness has become part of my life, and has influenced me a great deal throughout my illness. It's been a very good way of training me to live in the present and to keep little important things in mind every day.

As the weeks went by, I was starting to get stronger. I put on more weight, and I felt a lot better both physically and mentally. I started to do the things I used to enjoy before, like coaching at the rugby club, watching rugby matches with Becky, Siôn and Ianto and spending time with Lois, Owen and Beca, although Owen still found it hard to talk about my illness. Once again, I was feeling strong and was making the most of my life – which seemed miraculous.

After a Sound Healing session

༺ঌ

I was involved with Irfon's journey and treatment from the beginning, I'm sure, and although it wasn't a journey either one of us had imagined or wished for, it's been, in a strange way, a positive, jolly and inspiring one. Life affirming, you might say.

I first noticed that something was wrong at a New Year's Eve party in some friends' house at the end of 2013. There was no sign of Irfon in the large kitchen where we'd all congregated although the party was in full swing – he'd sneaked through to the living room with a soft drink as he had pains in his side. He wasn't quite himself, but as the evening went on he warmed up, telling us his rugby stories until everyone was laughing heartily at the local raconteur.

I saw him on the schoolyard a few days later, where he broke the news that shadows had shown up on a scan of his organs. In a matter of days, following further tests, the confirmation came that he had bowel cancer, and that it was likely to have already spread to the liver. I was gobsmacked.

I went to visit him that evening to try to raise his spirits, although I was in shock and had no idea what to say to him. But when he opened the door I saw the usual smile on his face, as if the doctor had only told him he had a zit on his bum which could be cured with a dab of Germolene! It was then that I realised that he was made of much sterner stuff than most of us.

From the off he had a positive outlook on the situation he'd found himself in. Despite the utter unfairness, I never heard him pity himself, and not once did he ask 'why me?' – he took everything in his stride and looked after the interests of his loved ones – his wife, children and close family. There was a determination in his eyes and his voice from the very beginning that he would beat and survive the horrid cancer that had invaded his body.

It would take a lot more that a few abnormal cells to break this former rugby captain's spirit ... a hell of a lot more. However, during his heroic battle against this horrible unrelenting disease, he had to fight just as hard against the government and health boards for the rights of cancer patients in Wales. Despite the clear evidence that Cetuximab could have saved his life in the early stages of his battle, his request for it was refused three times following several appeals over twelve months. A whole year of fighting against the system whilst the cancer was making headway in his organs.

His campaigning work through #Hawl i Fyw is well known by now, but many who have followed his story from the sidelines don't realise is that it was never a personal battle (it was already too late for Irfon to be treated in Wales) but a campaign to ensure that future cancer patients in Wales would never again have to face such unfairness as a result of the Welsh government's flawed policy.

He could have moved to England much sooner to save himself, but it was far more important to this patriotic Welshman to shed light on the scandal that existed beneath the surface of the health policy at the time. Not everyone could have mustered the strength to pit themselves against the system whilst fighting cancer, but he felt he had to act. I'm not sure what makes someone a hero – but I'm positive that Irfon's actions were heroic to say the least.

When the news came that the government had listened to the campaign's message, and that they accepted their policy's flaws, the jubilation on his face spoke volumes – not one person would again be failed like he was. Without a doubt, our debt to him, as a nation, is tremendous.

How would I describe the experience of watching his personal and political battles? With admiration, respect and disbelief at his bravery, I have to admit. When his journey started he was a physically large man. By the end he looked a lot smaller but was mentally head and shoulders above everyone else, a giant in his family and friends' eyes and a Welsh hero.

The news that he was to be ordained into the Gorsedd of the Bards at the Welsh National Eisteddfod was fantastic – as a Welshman he couldn't have received a higher honour. He was looking forward to the ceremony, but he passed away some two months before the Eisteddfod – which is ironic as 2017 marked the death of one of Wales' greatest poets, Hedd Wyn, who died in the First World War before being awarded his Bardic Chair. Irfon's legacy will be a lasting one, and patients in Wales will benefit from his actions for decades to come, safe in the knowledge that they too have a fighting chance.

Aled Prys, friend

Chapter 11

A Step Forward

In May 2016 the Assembly Elections were held, with Labour victorious once again. The work of #HawliFyw #FightingChance had obviously carried on – mainly because of my firm belief that the IPFR (Individual Patient Funding Request) system was inadequate for patients' needs. Former Health Minister Mark Drakeford had not been part of any discussion so far, and neither had he agreed to meet us during his period in the post, but by 2016 he'd been succeeded by Vaughan Gething.

Meeting Vaughan Gething

Quite out of the blue, we received a letter from him inviting us to discuss #HawliFyw #FightingChance with him, and to share our strong feelings about the policy. The Government had announced funds of £80 million to pay for treatments considered as 'exceptional' in Wales, and I'd given my opinion on the development on the media and in the press. I advised people not to celebrate too much and to carefully consider their response to this new money – because, of course, the only way of getting access to the money was by using the IPFR system, which hadn't changed. I knew from personal experience that steering a path through that policy was extremely difficult, and had heard the same story from individuals in the same situation as me throughout Wales. Of course, the negative impact that the process had on patients and their families created added stress during a period that was already difficult enough.

Becky and I immediately accepted the invitation, and a meeting was arranged at the Welsh Government office in Llandudno Junction on 13 June 2016. We were itching to know what Vaughan Gething had in mind.

At the meeting, he was very anxious to make us aware of what was being discussed in the Assembly about the plans that were in the pipeline. We at #HawliFyw #FightingChance had called for a cross-party response to the situation, as solving the current problem was something that went over and above politics. We'd had previous discussions, as I've already mentioned, with Andrew R.T. Davies of the Conservatives and Leanne Wood and Hywel Williams of Plaid Cymru calling for their support, and Elin Jones, the Assembly President, had expressed her support for a cross-party response to the issue.

To our surprise, Vaughan Gething gave us his word that he would assemble an independent panel charged with reviewing the IPFR policy, looking at the available information and producing guidelines, if necessary, for the restructuring of the policy and its implementation in Wales across all health boards. He proposed that the panel should be a truly independent one, whose members would be experienced individuals in the fields of business and health.

In September 2016 the Government announced that the panel had been established. It was chaired by a man called Andrew Blakeman, who worked for BP and was also an accountant. He was evidently a very intelligent man – he'd been a member of the NHS Transplant Services Board in England for eight years. He'd also been a cancer sufferer himself since 2000.

The rest of the panel members were just as eminent: Professor Peter Littlejohns (campaigner and professor of Public Health at King's College, London, who had worked for NICE), Professor Phil Routledge OBE (former chair of the all-Wales Medicines Strategy Group), Dr Ben Thomas (Medical director of Betsi Cadwaladr University Health Board and renal consultant), Professor Chris Newdick (barrister and professor of Health Law at Reading University... and a Mr Irfon Williams, who was described as a former Senior Nurse with personal experience of the IPFR process.

Despite feeling quite intimidated on reading about the other panel members, and feeling that my experience could never compete with the other men's vast knowledge, I quickly decided that it was a tremendous privilege to be chosen to represent patients throughout Wales, in order to ensure a strong voice for service users. I'd had experience of speaking at various patients' conferences, including one in particular in Cardiff under the auspices of another campaign, One Voice for Wales. The leader of that campaign was a woman I respected greatly: Annie Mulholland, who had experienced a very similar problem to mine during her own cancer journey; but I was still nervous. On the other hand, I felt quite excited too, and started to read as much as I could about IPFR policies and its history, and to invite some of the people who had contacted me about the matter to give their opinions. My intention was to use their evidence, as well as my own experience, as proof of what needed changing.

Meanwhile, I was feeling quite well, both physically and mentally. I was getting stronger every day, was even eating better, and the energy levels were rising. Sian Morgan Lloyd and Rhys Edwards, independent television producers who were working on behalf of ITV, had started following my progress some time before for the new documentary about me for the

O'r Galon series on S4C. They and the camera were now following me on a regular basis, focusing on my personal story rather than my campaigning work, in order to create a document of my life as I faced everything that my situation threw at me. I felt it was important to create a visual document of my situation – a sort of summary of this book, in a way – to give people a taste of what life was like for me during quite a turbulent year.

I was glad to be feeling so well, and to have bounced back from the surgery, which had been quite nasty. I remember one of my friends joking that the Grim Reaper was fed up with me because I always got better every time he came to get me! In fact, it was my faith in myself – and that of my family, friends and carers – as well as my resolute attitude, that influenced my health and recovery.

The biggest problem I had by that point was the colostomy – which was a sign, perhaps, that everything else had recovered very well. I had two enormous hernias on my belly, one on each side, and they weren't at all attractive. The one on the left seemed to be a lot bigger than the other, and on top of the hernia was the colostomy itself, which prolapsed and swelled up making it very difficult to treat. This caused a few unpleasant experiences. Once, when I was in a lift in a Cardiff hotel in the company of two strangers, a young couple, I broke wind in a big way (there was no routine or warning of the breaking wind!) and I had no way of explaining the situation to them. The look on their faces was priceless! They both shook their heads, surely thinking that I'd been brought up in a pigsty! On another occasion, during a meal in the company of friends, one of the bags burst, making quite a mess, to put it nicely. I had to go home alone to wash and get changed. Al Prys has the gift of making light of every situation with his humour, and he sent a message to everyone who'd been out with us that night saying that I was the biggest party pooper ever (in more ways than one ...)!

As I accepted more and more work through my new company, Hanner Llawn, I was increasingly nervous about how the colostomy would behave. One day, during a workshop in a local primary school, I eminated a hell of a lot of wind which was, of course, extremely funny to a group of eleven-year-olds! There was uproarious laughter, and there was nothing I could do about it except apologise. Unfortunately, that spectacular sight is on record as Rhys and Sian were there filming me!

My worst mishap happened when I was running a workshop during a secondary teachers' training day in Anglesey. The bag decided to burst once again. I evacuated far more from the bowels than usual, for some reason, and my shirt and jumper started getting soiled. I didn't know whether anyone else had noticed, but the workshop had half an hour to go. I picked up a book and held it in front of me in an attempt to hide the mess, hoping that I was far enough away from my audience for them not to notice the smell that was now filling my nostrils. At the end of the session I rushed out, shouting 'thanks very much for listening ...' over my shoulder, forgetting to leave them an invoice or anything! I'm sure they thought I'd completely lost the plot.

About mid-September I received a phone call from Mr Paul Skaiff's secretary – he was the surgeon who operated on my bowel at Aintree. He invited me to go to Aintree hospital to reverse the colostomy – a procedure which was, by all accounts, a fairly easy and successful one. As you can imagine, I was thrilled to bits, and although Becky wasn't too sure about it, she understood how much it meant to me. I'd already discussed it with Mr Malik, who felt that my quality of life would improve enormously if I could live without a colostomy. His opinion was that I should go for it. I'd never disagreed with Mr Malik before, and as he was now the only person I could consider to be a hero of mine, I wouldn't dream of going against his suggestion. The little things that I was used to taking for granted before, like reading the newspaper on the toilet, were impossible for me with the colostomy, and I was dreaming of getting back to 'normality' after two long years.

The intention was that I would spend three to five days in hospital. The intestine would be stitched back together and reinserted under the skin, and once the doctors were happy that it had started working again, I could go home.

Before I went into the hospital to reverse the colostomy, Becky and I had an honest talk about her concerns. She felt that my health was better than it had been in a long time, and disagreed with Mr Malik that the op was the best option for me. I understood her concerns, but nevertheless, I was adamant that I was going to put my faith, once again, in the specialist. Fair play to her, although she was very reluctant, Becky supported my decision in the end, and off I went to Liverpool for the operation, which was to take place on 4 October 2016.

By nine o'clock that morning I was in theatre. When I came round from the anaesthetic Becky was standing at my bedside, telling me that they hadn't been able to perform the operation, and my heart sank. She explained that the intestine was too narrow due to scar tissue to be rejoined together. If the surgery had gone ahead, it could have caused me serious chronic problems and left me constipated. Consequently, Mr Skaiff had spent an hour in the theatre inserting a tube through the intestine (down the colostomy and up my bottom) and inflating some kind of balloon inside it in order to widen the intestine. If that succeeded in proving that the intestine was strong enough, he was willing to try the colostomy reversal again two days later.

I was taken back to Ward 4 to await a scan the next morning. That scan proved to be brutal – it wasn't a normal scan, but entailed pumping five litres of fluid into my intestine through a tube (yes, up my bum again ...) to gauge the success of the previous day's balloon. Trying to keep all the liquid in was a very uncomfortable experience! The procedure was managed by a woman from Northern Ireland, and as Wales had beaten them at football in the European Championships a few months earlier she started pulling my leg that it was payback time for that defeat!

Mr Skaiff was satisfied with the scan results, and it was arranged for me to return to the theatre the next day for the colostomy reversal. After the operation, the intestine went into spasm (it's called 'lazy bowel', and the same thing had happened after my previous operations), and this obviously affected my ability to eat once again. Previously, this had lasted up to a week, and was a horrible feeling: I was unable to eat and regularly bringing up bile, as the bowel tried to prevent food from passing through it. Once again I had to have a nasogastric tube from my nose down to my stomach in order to collect any bile that was trapped there. This wasn't a pleasant feeling, but at least the throwing up was easier to deal with. The side-effect was that I couldn't eat, at a time when I was losing weight very rapidly anyway.

My favourite nurses, Ann and Tina, were still treating me like a king, doing far more than their usual duties for me. I started thinking of them as two modern-day female St Davids who 'did the little things', as the Patron Saint of Wales preached. Although I wasn't supposed to drink anything, they'd both go to the shop regularly to buy me an ice lolly (or 'lolly ice' as they called them) to suck on to keep my mouth from drying up. I can't describe what a wonderful feeling that was. Once, when the shop had run out of ice lollies, Ann went home especially to get some Tip-Tops for me instead!

At Aintree, as in all hospitals, there's a specific routine for every morning – they wake patients up early before the nurses stick their heads around the curtain at about 7 a.m. to say 'good morning' and distribute the breakfast trays. After that, usually, I'd be left in peace until washing time. Being very weak, I was given a bed bath by Ann, who was very gentle with me and washed every part of me thoroughly... apart, of course, from the 'privates'. She used to say to me, 'I think the world of you, babes, but I wouldn't go that far!'

Whenever another Welsh speaker landed on the ward, Ann and Tina would make sure they got the two of us together for about half an hour at a time, to give us a chance to converse in Welsh, realising the importance of our mother tongue to us. Tina always introduced me to the other patients like this: 'This guy's a Welshman from Bangor and he's a Mockin Beedee!' Of course, she meant 'mochyn budr' (the welsh for 'dirty pig') – she'd picked up the odd Welsh phrase here and there!

A patient from Tal-y-bont near Bangor, called Morfydd, came in to see me one day, and I realised that I knew her and her family well. That was quite handy – when one of us had visitors, the other usually knew them too and could have a good chat with them. I found out that Paul McLennan, one of the Bangor rugby lads, had just undergone a back operation at Walton Hospital (which is attached to Aintree Hospital), so as we shared the same friends, those who came to visit one of us would come and see the other subsequently during visiting hours. I knew two other patients on the ward too – ones I'd befriended during our previous stays in hospital – namely Paul Wain and Steve. I still keep in touch with Paul but Steve very sadly passed away as a result of complications following surgery for a very similar cancer to mine.

My bowel wasn't working too brilliantly, and my belly swelled up to a fair size. I started to feel quite ill, and was moved to a room on my own behind the nurses' desk. The doctors were called to see me urgently. Ed Alabraba got there first, and the concern was evident in his voice. He told me without beating about the bush, 'I'm worried, Irfon. You haven't got many tokens left after all you've been through, but we can't leave you like this.' He sent me for a scan which showed that my stomach was filling up with a fluid that was obviously infected. The duty consultant came over, and without any delay I was taken back to theatre to try and sort out the problem. Meanwhile I'd managed to empty my bowels two or three times in the 'old-fashioned way' – but that experience hadn't been as magical as I'd dreamed of (although, obviously, it was better than passing faeces into a bag on the side of my belly).

That night, they operated on my bowel, and as far as I understood, things had gone as well as could be expected. The surgeon came to talk to me the following morning to explain that a hole had opened in the site of the original tumour because the intestine hadn't healed well enough. This meant that the colostomy had to be re-introduced. Furthermore, it would be impossible to attempt the same operation ever again, which meant that my colostomy was permanent. I felt a mixture of emotions, but the main one was that I'd put myself through all this for the sake of something that I didn't really need. I could have lived perfectly well with the colostomy without going for the operation – but on the other hand, I might have regretted my decision had I not gone for it, and might have dwelled on the missed opportunity to live a completely 'normal' life. The doctors had no regrets either, but Becky was annoyed about the situation, and felt that she should have tried harder to persuade me not to have the operation in the first place as I was living such a healthy life prior to that. I had a long chat with Gary, who agreed that I would have regretted not giving it a go.

After the colostomy was reinserted, my bowel went into a lazy spasm once again, and took some time to recover. The swelling in my belly was starting to subside, I started to eat better and had the tube taken out of my nose. After three weeks at Aintree arrangements were made for me to go home to Bangor. As you'd expect, I was very happy about this, but there was sadness too, as I realised that I would never again return to Aintree Hospital to the doctors and nurses who had become such good friends, because there was nothing else they could do for me. Everything possible had been done with regard to treating my bowel and liver.

Gary came to fetch me from Aintree the following day, 20 October, and despite the fact that I didn't feel too special, and looked even worse after losing so much weight, I went home anyway. On arriving at the house I was very weak – I nearly fell headlong into the lounge, and my stomach was making very strange noises, like a washing machine. Although it was really nice to be back in my own bed, I didn't sleep well that night; I kept tossing and turning, throwing up a little and feeling quite sick. Becky wasn't happy, so she called Lowri Jones, the specialist colostomy nurse at Ysbyty Gwynedd, who'd given me so much support throughout the journey. She wasn't willing to let me stay at home, so she arranged for me to be seen in the assessment department of the Surgery Unit in Ogwen Ward. My belly had swollen up again – I looked like a pregnant man, about to give birth! When I arrived, I had blood tests, my blood pressure was taken and all the other usual tests were done before they transferred me to a private room on Ogwen Ward. Ffion, my stepbrother Andrew's daughter, was a staff nurse on the ward, and I felt a great deal of pride as I watched her go about her duties, knowing how hard she'd worked to succeed in realising her dream of becoming a nurse. Mr Whiteley, the consultant surgeon, came to see me; he was obviously very experienced in his field. He'd done his homework on my case, anyway, and proposed transferring me back to Aintree, before emphasising that he was also more than happy to treat me himself in Bangor after receiving my notes and the scan results from Aintree.

After sending me for another scan, he came back to me to explain that there was a probable blockage in the bowel, and that no faeces were able to pass through it. There was a great risk of my developing an infection. In his opinion, all the operations I'd been through had created adhesions, or scar tissues, that had stuck together causing a blockage. Very often, he said, the swelling would subside sufficiently in the days following surgery to solve the problem naturally, and in order to avoid any further surgery he was going to keep an eye on me for three or four days.

I started vomiting again, and had to have a tube from my nose to my stomach once again, and a urine catheter in order to monitor the kidneys and make sure that my body didn't become dehydrated. But despite this, my condition was deteriorating. Boils and blisters, obviously infected, started to develop along my belly and side, seeming to follow the scars of the old operations. Some of these burst, emitting a mixture of yellow fluid and blood.

Mr Whiteley was called immediately, and without any delay he took me to theatre to wash the scars, reopen some of them and cleanse them thoroughly with a strong antibiotic before taking me back to the ward to start on another intravenous course of strong antibiotics into a vein in my neck and into the PICC line that had been inserted in my arm a few days earlier. There was nothing else that could be done except wait for me to start getting better. I was very glad that Mr Whiteley had decided to feed me a special nutrient fluid through the PICC line, putting great emphasis on giving me albumen, a special protein that strengthened me and healed the body more quickly. As a result, I didn't lose any more weight and I'm very grateful to him for that. I got on well with Mr Whiteley, even though Becky wasn't convinced, and I feel enormous gratitude to him and his medical team. Once more, the nurses on the ward were exceptionally kind to me. One of them, Christine

'Bach', reminded me of Ann in Aintree. I was still in the hospital come Halloween night, and Christine came to me before finishing her shift that day with two bags of sweets, for me to give one each to Siôn and Ianto (I was expecting them in their fancy dress to give me a fright) and a bottle of wine for me to give to Becky, so that she could relax a little once the boys had gone to bed, after having had to suffer several days of worry on my account.

During my last stay at Aintree, Mr Skaiff had found lumps on the outside of the intestine, and nodules that appeared to be loose in the area of my pelvis and abdomen. He'd taken samples of these but I was sent home before the results came back. Mr Skaiff was aware of my present situation as Mr Whiteley had asked for every bit of information about me from Aintree, so when the results came back, he immediately contacted Mr Whiteley to break the news to him.

Mr Whiteley and one of his colleagues came to my room on the afternoon of 1 November, to tell me that Mr Skaiff had confirmed that the cancer had spread, which explained the lumps. So, by that point, the original cancer which started in the bowel had spread to the liver, the lungs and now to the pelvic cavity and the outer wall of the small intestine. I'd already made enquiries about lung surgery at Broadgreen, and after Becky and I discussed the matter at length, we'd come to the conclusion that it wouldn't be a viable option for me. It would have entailed more than three months' treatment on each lung, and I wanted to focus on living my life, and make the most of each day. This decision, again, had been made for me, in effect. I told Becky that night what Whiteley had confirmed. I could see that she was shocked, although she did her best to hide it from me.

I was on Ogwen ward in Ysbyty Gwynedd until mid-November. We were supposed to go down to Cardiff to see

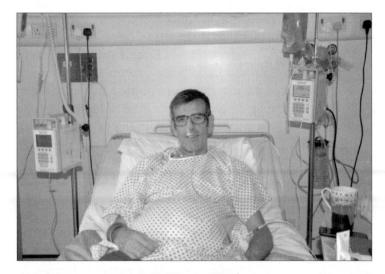

On Ogwen Ward

Wales play rugby in the autumn internationals, but I wasn't well enough to go, so Becky brought my Wales scarf into hospital for us to watch the match there together.

While I was on Ogwen I received an alarming message from Siôn via his ipad. He said that Becky had fallen at home – she'd collapsed with chest pains and an ambulance had brought her in to casualty. I went down to meet her there. It had been caused by stress, according to the doctors, and fortunately, she was allowed to go home later that day. I came home later that week, although I was still on intravenous antibiotics. Oddly enough, I was due to go to Venue Cymru in Llandudno to present an award at the Betsi Cadwaladr Staff Awards on the day I came home – I was tired, but at least I managed to go – and got a chance to thank the NHS staff for everything they'd done for me.

We'd bought tickets for the Wales v Japan rugby match on 19 November, and although I'd only just come out of hospital, I was determined to take Ianto to his first rugby international.

We had a great weekend, but as we were on our way home, around Builth Wells, I started to feel unwell. Becky and I strongly suspected that I had another infection, and although we discussed changing our route in order to reach a hospital with an A&E department, I was determined to get back to Bangor. Becky took me to Ysbyty Gwynedd straight away, even before going home, and I was taken immediately to Ogwen Ward once again, to be put on antibiotics for a few days.

By the end of November I was home once again, and preparing for Christmas with the family. I was very happy to be able to attend the boys' Christmas shows. I managed to get tickets to go to Anfield to see Liverpool play West Ham on 11 December – Ianto loves football and Liverpool FC in particular, so I was very glad that I'd had a chance to take him.

I was still trying to recover after the last treatment, and was pleased to see how quickly the scars were healing. But although the scars were healing well I looked terribly ill – my face looked too small for my nose and ears, and I was terribly thin. One or

Siôn and Ianto at Anfield for the first time

two people didn't even recognise me! This was the result of the eating problems, of course, and something had to be done about it straight away, or it would have killed me. The issue developed into a source of tension between Becky and I, and it affected the boys too, while I was in the middle trying to eat but not being able to. No-one seemed to understand the situation from my viewpoint – and I wondered if they thought I was doing it on purpose. Through trying to eat small portions of food often, the situation started to slowly improve, and in time I was able to eat stuff like porridge. I started eating things I'd have avoided in the past, fatty foods that aren't too healthy, but they helped me to put on weight. I considered trying one or two not-so-legal substances too ... but in the end I wasn't tempted!

We had a number of Christmas parties with friends and I managed to go to them all, but never managed to eat the meals. Of course, in rugby parties and so on there was no shortage of mouths to eat the leftover food – and Becky was able to enjoy herself in the knowledge that she wouldn't have to drive home!

That Christmas day we went to Becky's parents' in Penrhyn Bay. Dad came with us too, as otherwise he'd have been on his own in Caernarfon. We had a very good day, and all the rest of the family joined us for the evening. The next day we went to Mam and Clive's in Talwrn with Lois, Owen and Beca – that was one tradition I wasn't going to break.

Becky's parents bought us a trip to Jersey as a Christmas present – I'd always wanted to go there. Becky had spent some of her formative years living on the island, and I'd wanted to see the place having heard her talk fondly about it. The day before we left I'd intended to take the boys for a walk to Newborough beach (despite Becky's protests) to let her finish taking down the Christmas decorations. I didn't get very far – I stepped out of the door and fell flat on my face after tripping over Christmas lights! I looked a real sight as we started off for

The 'Soup and Song' evening

Jersey, but we had a really good time, in spite of my appearance and the fact that I was still vomiting regularly. I had to hire a mobility scooter at the zoo because I was so tired, but the boys had great fun having a spin on it. Of course, Becky had to tease me that I was like one of the characters in the TV series *Benidorm*!

My family and friends started to get used to the fact that there was no curing the cancer. Of course, no-one knew exactly what that meant, but my friends were agreed that they were going to arrange plenty of fun and games for me.

Harri Pritchard, my old school friend who's now a GP, got together with Rhys Meirion to organise a 'Cawl a Chân' (Soup and Song) party at Tŷ Golchi café near Bangor on 13 January 2017. Comedian Tudur Owen gave us a sample of his very funny show, Elin Fflur sang as beautifully as always and Rhys had great fun embarrassing us all by making us perform one of his trademark songs, 'Anfonaf Angel', in coloured wigs (while failing to hit any of the top notes!). That was one of the best nights I've ever had, in such a relaxed and happy atmosphere surrounded by family and friends. Nick, a nursing friend of mine from many years ago, arranged a reunion of the old gang from Ysbyty Gwynedd Social Club, which, as I've previously said, was a brilliant place. We all had loads of laughs that night, singing and dancing.

On 11 February a few of us went down to Cardiff for a school friends' reunion. The gang consisted of Andy, Alan, Tremayne and Robin, who lives in Cardiff these days. We went to the Wales v England rugby match that Saturday afternoon, which was one of the best games I've ever attended. Our seats were right next to the coaching team (thanks to Robin's contacts), and we stayed at the players' hotel. We had a fantastic night of reminiscing, and everyone except me was very drunk – I was on the coffee all night! We had another trip to Cardiff a few weeks later to see Siôn take part in a Flashmob with

Robin, Tremayne, me, Andy and Alan in Cardiff

Glanaethwy Choir – he was one of the youngest members of the choir and I, of course, was very proud of him.

Throughout all this, Rhys and Sian were still following me with the camera, filming material for the documentary. The filming ended in February 2017 with a rugby trip in the company of friends to Rome, and the programme was broadcast in May. I wasn't well during that rugby trip, but I was determined to go. Becky and I spent a lot of our time in the hotel – we'd been to the city before, so there was no pressure to go and see all the famous sights – but we still had a lot of fun.

Although Rhys Meirion complains that the quality of his singing on the rugby trip didn't come across very well on television, the *O'r Galon* programme was a really good one in my opinion, and I got a tremendous response to it. It showed the personal side of my life, rather than the campaigner and political figure, something that was very important to me. Now there's a record on film (and on paper too by now, thanks to this book) of me as a man of flesh and blood, whose journey has included tears as well as laughter. These will be mementoes for my children forever.

Despite having started to put on weight I was still vomiting frequently, and it was decided that something would have to be done about it. I saw a psychiatrist on Hergest ward, Ysbyty Gwynedd, for his opinion about the suggestion that the problem's origins might be psychological. I got the same attitude from him as I'd experienced from many before, namely, 'You've got cancer – what do you expect?' This always disappointed and infuriated me to some extent. In my opinion, it's important to try and solve every problem that accompanies cancer, to the utmost of our ability.

I had an appointment with a consultant on Alaw Ward in March 2017, who put me on a small course of steroids. Believe

Being interviewed for Radio 4's Money Box

it or not, in three days I was eating like a horse! Although the drugs had some pretty nasty side-effects – weakening the arm and leg muscles, for example – I felt very well, to be honest.

The press and media were still showing an interest in my situation, and over the following months I spoke on radio and television about my personal situation, the task of raising awareness of cancer issues in Wales and raising money – in Wales and beyond. I did interviews for *Money Box* on Radio 4 and Radio 5 Live, and an interview with the *Guardian* about the changes to widows' pensions. The last interview I did was *Heno* on 5 May, after having a blood transfusion. Despite being exhausted, I was pleased to be able to give a voice to patients throughout Wales and beyond about the additional worries that arise from a cancer diagnosis, the pains which stretch way beyond the physical ones.

Finishing writing this book with Nia, my editor

֎

Five words come to my mind when I think about Dad: brave, hero, supportive, loving and funny.

We have very happy memories of our childhood with Dad. He always looked on the bright side, no matter what. We relied on him for a bit of ribbing, but he excelled at embarrassing us in unexpected situations! Every morning when he left me at Ysgol Llanfairpwll primary school he insisted I give him a farewell kiss, which, for a young girl, was extremely embarrassing. Following that, he used to dance along the pavement as he made his way home, singing 'When You Ask About Love' by Matchbox on the top of his voice as he went.

Dad was an incredible influence on myself, Owen and Beca, and encouraged us, whatever we turned our hands to. We will always remember his strong love of music. Owen and I started playing the Tenor horn when we were about seven, and I joined Beaumaris Brass Band, with Dad at my side playing the euphonium. Beca and Siôn have obviously inherited his musicality. Beca is a very talented piano and flute player and Siôn Arwyn really enjoys singing. Recently, he won first prize in his school's talent contest and he's a proud member of Glanaethwy Choir. This meant that every trip in the car was more like a karaoke session, everyone singing their parts in harmony.

I spent many Saturdays at the rugby ground supporting Dad and his friends. His love of rugby was always evident, and Ianto has followed in his footsteps. Unfortunately, Owen always preferred football, so Dad formed and coached the Hotshots for several years when Owen was younger. They won quite a few games because of Dad's support and devotion, and I know that many of the players still have a soft spot for him.

The day Dad broke the news to us about his illness is still a bit fuzzy. Three years later, we're still finding it difficult. It's been an extremely hard journey for us as a family. There was nothing worse that seeing Dad, who used to be so strong and healthy, in pain and suffering. A weak, empty feeling. But despite this, he succeeded in inspiring and supporting us, his children, with his positivity.

Seeing Dad cope with living with cancer has been an inspiration to me, Owen and Beca. Although he was the one suffering, he's been an immense help to other patients and their families by fundraising for #teamIrfon and raising awareness about access to cancer treatments through #Fighting Chance. All of this, and all the other amazing things he's accomplished throughout his life, make it an honour for us to call him 'Dad'. Siôn and Ianto are a bit young to fully understand everything at the moment, but when they are a little older, it will be our honour to share his story with them.

Dad has left a gaping hole in our lives and we can't help thinking about the future – the little things such as the fact that he won't be with us on our wedding days, won't see Beca, Siôn and Ianto become adults, won't see his grandchildren. When the time comes, we'll share his story with them, too! But one thing is certain: his legacy lives on in all of us, and his heart and spirit will be with us always.

Lois

Chapter 12

Hawl i Fyw / Fighting Chance

One of the things I'm proudest of, as I look back, is what my journey has achieved. I've never been a political animal, and at one time I followed in the footsteps of my Caernarfon grandparents, who were staunch Labour supporters as Taid had been a quarryman all his life. I'm sure they didn't realise that I used to listen to every word they said at the dinner table when I was a child! Mam and Dad were Conservatives years ago – which was even worse!

I started to become aware of Welsh nationalism at Ysgol y Garnedd in Bangor, and as I grew older, I started to learn more about politics and tried to understand policies that affected Wales. Since then, I've taken an interest in the subject, and believe strongly in the principles and campaigns of Plaid Cymru. I believe this was an advantage during my cancer journey, and I also strongly believe that the personal health of individuals and families is a far more important issue than the tenets of any individual political party.

The aim of #HawliFyw #FightingChance right from the very start was to influence the political parties in Wales in order to change the present system, and that's been a success. After Elin Jones's appointment as President of the Welsh Assembly in 2016, we received a letter signed by her and the leaders of the political parties undertaking to all work together to improve the situation with regard to accessing drugs in Wales. I was very pleased when Vaughan Gething was appointed Health Minister – his predecessor, Mark Drakeford, hadn't been very open during our campaign (apart from sending one letter, containing inaccurate facts) and had avoided meeting us.

As I've already mentioned, I felt very privileged when I was invited to be part of the independent panel to discuss the IPFR policy. I had to build up confidence and be certain of my facts in order to discuss with the other members, and I learnt a great deal during that period. I'm very grateful for the other members' willing support, especially the chairman, Andrew Blakeman, who made sure that I was aware of what was happening throughout the discussion process and who promised me that the process would not be dragged out. He was as good as his word. The panel made 27 recommendations regarding the IPFR policy, which were submitted in very concise draft document form. After everyone had submitted their comments on this, the final document was submitted to the Government.

In March 2017 I was informed that Vaughan Gething was going to give an address in the Senedd to present the conclusions of the independent panel. I was delighted – and smiled broadly – when he announced that every one of the 27 recommendations had been approved, and were to be implemented in every health board throughout Wales by September 2017. I was aware that #HawliFyw #FightingChance had very strongly influenced the policy, and that all my hard work had borne fruit.

So, not only have we succeeded in influencing the availability of the Cetuximab drug in Wales, but far more importantly in my opinion, the policy is going to be much fairer, more open and easier to read from now on. Families who are in the same situation as we were, families who are going through a turbulent time, will find it easier to deal with the administrative side. When I had to fight for the right to get a drug that would alleviate my situation, I felt angry and frustrated at having to go through a system that debased and degraded me. It won't be like this from now on, I hope.

From a personal viewpoint, I hope that I as an individual have been able to show strength, and that we as a family have responded to our situation with dignity, even though it would have been easy enough for me to go quietly to England to receive my treatment without considering the needs of others in the same situation as myself. But that isn't my nature. The fact that my experience has benefitted so many other people throughout Wales gives me great comfort, and makes me feel very happy. When someone comes up to me in the street and shakes my hand, sometimes in tears, thanking me for all my work, I feel that I've done my little bit for Wales.

Yes, I've received several awards for what I've done, and I'm very proud of them all – the Leader of the Year Award from Bangor University and the *Daily Post*, Champion of Champions from the Trinity Mirror company and awards from the Health Board – but the one that brought most tears to my eyes was the special Inspiration prize from Llanfairpwll football club.

On 11 April 2017, I came home after a day out with the family to find a letter from the Gorsedd of Bards on the doormat. The Gorsedd is an association linked with the Welsh National Eisteddfod, comprising of poets, writers, musicians, artists and other people who have made a distinguished contribution to the Welsh nation, the language, and its culture. The letter announced that I'd been made a member of the Gorsedd for my work in raising awareness of health issues. Well, I couldn't believe it. I cried that day too. An honour from the Queen would mean nothing to me, but to be honoured like this by my country was the biggest privilege I can imagine. I thought immediately about my dear friend Robin McBryde who had already been accepted into the Gorsedd – two of Ysgol Tryfan's naughty lads on the National Eisteddfod field in their gowns! I've chosen my poetic name – it wasn't a difficult decision – Irfon o'r Hirael, which simply refers to where I grew up.

I've had the privilege of meeting some incredible people and making new friends along my journey, including patients, NHS staff here in Wales, in Liverpool and Manchester, and other individuals who have inspired me. One of these is Mr Malik, who's become a bit of a hero to me. Having said that, there's a tendency, in my opinion, to use the word 'hero' a little too often these days. I would never consider myself a hero. Yes, I'm proud of myself and of Becky, as well as those people who have worked behind the scenes to campaign and spread the message about #HawliFyw #FightingChance. I'm extremely proud that Awyr Las raised over £150,000 in such a short time – quite an achievement when you consider that the original target was just £20,000. The heroes in this instance are the children, young people, and the hundreds, if not thousands, of people who don't know me at all but who have collected various and incredible sums of money for the cause – be it by running six marathons in six days or by selling half a dozen cakes on the school yard. This has all given me great pleasure.

Everyone hopes they'll influence their families and make a positive impression on them. Every parent, I suppose, wants to see their children grow up to be adults and make their own way in life. I know I won't get that privilege. But I believe that I've influenced the personalities of Lois, Owen, Beca, Siôn and Ianto. I've been worried about Owen's ability to cope with my illness and I feel so glad that in the past month or two he's turned a corner and has managed to talk openly with me about the cancer and about death, and has been brave enough to cry with me, to hold me and to talk about anything, for once, other than Liverpool football club! One day, I hope the five of them will sit down together and talk about Dad – how ridiculous he was sometimes, how he made everyone laugh and how embarrassing he could be! I hope they'll be able to sit back and consider what I would have said to them, whatever the situation may be. I hope the five of them will develop strength from somewhere to deal with everything life throws at them, and that they'll be able to ask the question, 'What would Dad do now?' when they need guidance. I want them to be confident and strong, and to develop the ability to challenge what they perceive to be wrong, especially after the experience I've had.

I also hope that everyone who's aware of my story will learn from my experience: don't accept what politicians or doctors tell you. Go and look for your own answers. After all, everyone has a right to live. Everyone deserves a Fighting Chance.

The last selfie

Acknowledgements

It would take me forever to name everyone who has supported me through this journey. You all know who you are, and you've made a tremendous difference to me.

I must, however, at this point, thank those who have helped me with this book:

Becky for her patience and her ability to drive me

Nia for her support, and for putting me on the right track when I lost my focus

Mam, Dad and Clive for searching for photographs

Tegwen Alaw for the hours spent typing in my company

Everyone who wrote kind words about me

Epilogue

Irfon's health took a sudden turn for the worse on 6 May 2017. That morning he didn't wake up as he usually would to have breakfast with the family, and he was very drowsy. As he tried to get downstairs mid morning he sat on a stair half way down, put his head in his hands and cried. 'I'm dying now,' he said, and we looked at each other in desperation. For the first time I saw real vulnerability. I tried to reassure him that this was another blip in his health and we would get it sorted, however I felt the terror rise as I knew Irfon just knew. The following day Irfon was admitted to hospital and by the next morning he was unconscious. I had a meeting with the Palliative care team who explained that he had entered a new phase of the illness and was now at the end of his life, words I never ever wanted to hear. Irfon and I had discussed what he wanted at the end of life – we both agreed that he should be at our home with the family. This meant that we could still be together as a family unit and keep our routine going as much as possible for the boys. In line with our plan, and still unconscious, Irfon was transferred home by ambulance that afternoon. The family and close friends were informed and we all had an opportunity in turn to say our goodbyes; the Reverend Kathy visited and performed last rites.

That night, a Marie Curie Nurse came to the house to sit with Irfs whilst I attempted to rest. At about 2am I could hear chatting and laughing so I got up and went into our bedroom where the nurse and Irfon were. To my astonishment Irfon was propped up in bed showing the nurse photos on his phone. He was in full swing, reeling off a funny story and she was laughing – he'd even asked her to make him a cup of tea. All I could say was 'What the Hell is going on?' Irfon looked at me, confused, and said, 'What? I wanted a cup of tea!' I couldn't quite process that we had gone from an unconscious Irfon having his last rites and us all saying goodbye to now seeing him sitting up in bed telling jokes. I explained what had happened over the previous couple of days and he said he had no recollection of it, but was determined he wasn't ready to die just yet – he said he had a book to finish first! Even the medics who had said he only had hours left to live were surprised by this turnaround – however, as one doctor said to me '… mind you, this is Irfon we're talking about!'

Over the next few weeks, although mainly confined to his bed, we were able to spend quality time together as a family. Too weak to type but as determined as ever, Irfon dictated the last chapters of this book. He sorted through photos and left me a file on the laptop of the ones he wanted included. The cover of the book was speedily put together so he could see it and he was so proud to have this confirmation that his autobiography *would* be published. We all knew how important getting his story down was to Irfs, and so I became increasingly anxious that once he finished that, it would be his final mission complete. The extra time we had over those few weeks meant we were able to sit with the boys and share our most treasured memories of our time together. It was a heartbreaking but very special process. We cried, laughed (we always laughed!) and I lay with my head on his chest as I always did, whilst we talked about what we hoped for the future … a future without Irfon physically here. One day I broached the issue of his funeral. Irfon was never a planner, and he quipped, 'you sorted the wedding and I know you'll do a great job of the funeral!' but I was anxious to have his approval in advance; that way I'd have the reassurance of knowing everything was as it should be. Irfon asked me to ring an undertaker friend, Arwel 'Box', and so I picked up the phone and explained to Arwel that Irfon was very poorly and that we wanted to discuss funeral planning. We were so very grateful to Arwel for coming straight over, and we sat with him in the bedroom discussing the arrangements in a very matter of fact way. Irfon even joked that any large cardboard box would do as a coffin. Afterwards, Arwel told me he'd never been asked to have a meeting like that before, and felt so privileged. Everything was now in place.

On 26 May, Irfon began to experience excruciating pain in his abdomen and we were unable to relieve it despite extra doses of morphine. He was reviewed by the palliative care team who felt we couldn't manage his pain at home as he required more intensive nursing. The decision was made for us: Irfs was taken back to hospital by ambulance and made comfortable. A CT scan was performed that showed a blockage in his bowel caused by a tumour. Irfon didn't want to receive the details of the CT as he was feeling so unwell, so he asked me to talk to the doctors, then tell him. Breaking the news to him that there was nothing more medically that could be done was heartbreaking. We sat there hand in hand, his eyes looking back at me over his oxygen mask as he listened to what I had to say, and he knew he was going to take control. We agreed the priority now was for a 'good death', that being timely and pain free. This was it, that was our new hope and purpose.

The next few days I spent next to Irfon's bedside on Alaw ward and the boys visited morning and evening whilst being cared for by my parents. Irfon's parents, his older children and his brothers made rotational visits. A group of friends, feeling they wanted to be close, gathered for two consecutive nights in the hospital – a vigil for Irfon. Although we knew the outcome and Irfs slipped in and out of consciousness, I can't say the atmosphere was morbid. We managed to joke and smile whilst recounting humorous stories of our life with Irfon – I'm sure laughter was often heard coming from his room because that was how life was with Irfon. You always laughed when you were in his company, and he would have been very happy about that. On the afternoon of 30 May, Irfon fell into a deep unconscious state and whilst alone together that evening he took his last breath.

*   *   *

Life without Irfon has been very tough. The grief is extremely painful and we have to work very very hard to adjust and be happy. One thing death teaches you is that life is so precious and time moves very quickly; it's important to seize the moment and live life to the full. Irfon, if he lived another 46 years, would have continued to be the amazing person he always was, wanting to make life easier for others. Although Irfon is not here physically to do that, he hoped that by telling his story this book would carry on that work.

Irfon sent me a text in the week before his death, and I often read it for comfort. Although now alone physically, Irfon will always be with me. Life is steered by those special conversations we had during our life together, about hopes for our family's future. If I ever feel lost when I'm trying to make decisions I know I can always be guided by our unfaltering love. The children will always have a wonderful father who was so very, very proud of them. I've learnt death cannot ever take that away from us.

Becky